DUGOUTS

&

DIAMONDS

*Heartaches and Triumphs
With the Texas Rangers*

By Jim Reeves

BERKELEY PLACE BOOKS

Dugouts & Diamonds
Heartaches and Triumphs With the Texas Rangers

By Jim Reeves
Editor: Amy Culbertson
Book designer: Tom Johanningmeier
Cover designer: Kari Lindner Crane

© Copyright MMXXII by Jim Reeves
1st edition 10 9 8 7 6 5 4 3 2 1

ISBN 978-1-892588-708

Berkeley Place Books
An imprint of Great Texas Line Press
Post Office Box 11105
Fort Worth, Texas 76110
TEL 817-922-8929 / FAX 817-926-0420

COVER PHOTOS:

Front: Celebrating Nolan Ryan's record seventh no-hitter in 1991.
Photo by Ron Jenkins. Courtesy, Fort Worth Star-Telegram Collection, Special Collections, The University of Texas at Arlington Libraries

Back, top: Catcher Pudge Rodriguez with manager Johnny Oates.
© Texas Rangers

Back, bottom: A bloodied Nolan Ryan continues pitching after being hit by a Bo Jackson one-hopper in 1990.
© Linda Kaye, with permission from her family

Also by Jim Reeves
Dallas Cowboys: Legends of America's Team
Remember the Alamo Bowl: Bram Kohlhausen's Epic TCU Comeback

CONTENTS

ACKNOWLEDGEMENTS

PROJECTS LIKE THESE involve multiple interviews and help from dozens of sources. At the risk of forgetting someone, and in no real order, I need to thank those who were gracious in their contributions to this book.

John Blake, the hardest-working man in Texas Rangers history, was there with vital information, phone numbers, advice — and as a reliable sounding board. I'm not sure the franchise won't completely collapse the day he walks out the door.

Nolan Ryan and son Reese graciously sat down with me in Round Rock for a lunch that was rich in memories. Tom Grieve, Kathy Grieve, Rich Billings, Eric Nadel, Mark McLemore, Jim Sundberg, Buddy Bell, Reid Ryan and Bobby Valentine helped with phone interviews, some more than once. Parker Vandergriff, Viveca Vandergriff and former Rangers trainer Bill Zeigler were also spot-on with their contributions.

Newspaper colleagues Randy Galloway, Steve Pate, Paul Hagen, Phil Rogers, Gil LeBreton, Carlos Mendez and T.R. Sullivan kept me between the lines when my own memory strayed to one side or the other.

A fledgling sportswriter in Fort Worth-Dallas couldn't have had better role models than Blackie Sherrod, Frank Luksa and Galyn Wilkins. I absorbed everything I could from them.

Nolan Ryan graciously sat down with me in Round Rock for a lunch that was rich in memories. Tom Grieve, Rich Billings, Eric Nadel, Mark McLemore, Jim Sundberg, Buddy Bell and Bobby Valentine helped with phone interviews, some more than once. Parker Vandergriff, Viveca Vandergriff and former Rangers trainer Bill Zeigler were also spot-on with their contributions.

Newspaper colleagues Randy Galloway, Steve Pate, Paul Hagen, Phil Rogers and T.R. Sullivan kept me between the lines when my own memory strayed to one side or the other.

Newspaper, magazine and website archives from the *Fort Worth Star-Telegram, Dallas Morning News, Dallas Times-Herald, The Athletic, D Magazine* and *Texas Monthly* were incredibly helpful in keeping facts straight and providing accurate quotes on events as they happened.

Great Texas Line Press publisher Barry Shlachter showed remarkable forbearance and restraint as I missed occasional deadlines, something that never happened when I was covering the Rangers. Life has a way of making us play at its own pace as we get older.

My thanks and extreme appreciation to Amy Culbertson, whose editing skills were put to the test time and again. She has never failed to make me better.

Closer to home, thanks to my wife, Karen Reeves, for her infinite support and patience. For over 40 years she has been the rock that I lean on every day.

— *Jim Reeves, Arlington, Texas*

Introduction

THE DANCING BEAR

IT WAS DAVID ALLAN COE, with a little help from an old friend, who inadvertently branded me with the nickname "The Dancing Bear."

The man who sang "You don't have to call me darlin', darlin'" was the genesis of it, anyway. Recollections are a bit hazy, you understand, and not just because almost five decades have passed since that rather festive night in a Fort Lauderdale roadhouse.

An ensemble of baseball beat writers, players and assorted others from the 1977 Rangers spring camp at Pompano Beach, Fla., were feeling a bit rowdy as Coe and his band belted out his signature song, "You Never Even Called Me by My Name." The singer was getting plenty of help from the overflow crowd, an eclectic mix of baseball types in shorts and polos; shitkickers in boots and ten-gallon hats; and bikers decked out in leather and metal studs. It was a strange sing-along, to say the least.

The tension between the latter two fraternities was palpable, but that wasn't atypical for a David Allan Coe performance. Both groups claimed Coe as a soul brother but inevitably glared at each other in suspicion, trying to figure out how they could possibly have anything in common. It was an uneasy armistice, with testosterone running heavy in both camps.

Now and then there would be a commotion somewhere in the big room, and a squad of bouncers the size of the Cowboys' offensive line would swing into action. There would be no yellow flags for holding here: The offenders would be gently encouraged to take their business elsewhere, and things would settle down until the next disturbance.

The uncertain atmosphere wasn't enough to keep me off the dance floor, though. Inspired by the right music, the right atmosphere and ample amounts of barley and hops, I have frequently in my life followed the old adage and danced like no one was watching.

Except ... almost every time, somebody is.

On this occasion it was Randy Galloway, my partner in crime from the *Dallas Morning News,* sipping on a longneck and surveying the room as Coe and the band played their hit "Dakota, the Dancing Bear."

"Gawddam, Revo," he drawled as I lurched from the dance floor. "You *are* the gawddam Dancing Bear."

The nickname stuck; I suppose because it was a reasonably apt description of a human being shaped like a beer keg careening uncontrollably around the dance floor.

~ ~ ~

DANCING, FROM O'Lunney's in Manhattan to Fitzwilly's at Lauderdale-by-the-Sea to the Palomino in L.A., was just one of the many perks of traveling with the Rangers for me. The era of beat writers basically embedding themselves with a team, as we did with the Rangers back in the 1970s and '80s, has passed into history, just as the age of journalists traveling on trains with teams did before that. Those were extraordinary times that will never be repeated.

People have been urging me to write a book about what it was like covering the Rangers, as a beat writer and as a columnist, for some 35 years. I loved the idea, but at the same time it scared me. I didn't know where to start, where to wind things up. I had so much information, so many stories. The task seemed overwhelming.

Then I saw the Rangers' 50th anniversary approaching in 2022, and that inspired me, finally, to get serious about trying to capture what it has been like and what it has meant to me to have been an eyewitness to so much Rangers history.

What I'm attempting in the book you're about to read is to give readers an inside look at the team through the eyes of a baseball writer, while at the same time telling some stories about the characters that have danced — sometimes literally — across the Rangers' stage.

This is not a complete history of the Rangers, not by a long shot. What you'll read here are snapshots of some of the events and the people I believe have made the Rangers who and what they are over the years.

I retired from the *Fort Worth Star-Telegram* in November 2009 after 40-plus years that touched parts of five decades. It was typical bad timing on my part: The Rangers would finally get to the World Series the very next year. Fortunately, ESPN.com had hired me to write some columns, and I covered that 2010 Series for them.

In 2011, when the Rangers were back in the World Series against the St. Louis Cardinals, the *Star-Telegram* asked me to do some free-lance work during home games. That meant I was spared from watching the heartbreak of Game 6 in person — but, as most of you know, that didn't make it any less painful. It's still an open wound. I don't expect it will heal until the day the Texas Rangers become world champions.

Some boys dream of playing major-league baseball. Others, like me, understand their limitations and have abilities that lead in other directions. Covering the Rangers and major-league baseball as a journalist was the fulfillment of my dream.

I'd like to think that I took some of you along with me on that journey. In this book, I'd like to take you along for the ride as I revisit some of the high points of the trip.

At the least, I hope you'll hear the same music I heard and be moved to tap your toes along with it.

Chapter 1

THE FIRST HERO
Tom Vandergriff Had a Dream

TOM VANDERGRIFF WAS A MAYOR, a congressman, a judge and a highly successful businessman. What he wanted to grow up to be was Vin Scully, the Hall of Fame baseball announcer for the Los Angeles Dodgers. He had the talent, the charisma, the brains and the compassion to be president of the United States. Instead, he spent years fighting to bring major-league baseball to Arlington. This is how he did it.

IT WAS PITCH-DARK in Bob Short's closet. Arlington Mayor Tom Vandergriff couldn't see much, but he could hear the voices just beyond the door in Short's office. He could make out a few words here and there.

On the other side of the door, Short was in an intense conversation with none other than David Eisenhower, grandson of former president Dwight Eisenhower, son-in-law of current president Richard Nixon, namesake of the renowned presidential retreat Camp David.

Eisenhower's arrival had interrupted Vandergriff's own meeting with Short. They had been discussing details of how Short might move his major-league baseball team, the Washington Senators, to north Texas.

It was a steamy July day in 1971 in Washington, D.C., and Vandergriff could feel his shirt getting damp in the stuffy closet. He stood perfectly still, afraid to move lest he bump into something and make a sound.

It was an extremely awkward moment for the dignified mayor of Arlington, Texas, the city Vandergriff fervently hoped would soon be the new home of Short's Washington Senators. Here he was, hiding in a dark closet, while outside, Eisenhower, representing Nixon himself, was forcefully letting Short know how unhappy the president would be if the Senators abandoned the nation's capital.

What would happen if he was discovered, Vandergriff wondered. How embarrassing would that be? Tom could just imagine the young Eisenhower gleefully reporting back to his father-in-law that he'd caught that team-thieving mayor from Texas skulking in Short's closet. The Washington newspapers would have a field day with the story. It would become a national debacle that Vandergriff might never live down. It could scuttle his hopes of persuading Short to move his team to Texas.

Even worse, it would be a major embarrassment for Arlington, the city he loved more than anything. That would be unbearable.

But what else could he have done in the few seconds he and his host had been given to react?

When Short's secretary had announced that Eisenhower had shown up unexpectedly and wanted an immediate audience, both Vandergriff and Short were caught — well, short. There was no way Vandergriff could exit the office without running into Eisenhower, and that would not do. Short quickly suggested the closet as the only resort.

So here Vandergriff stood in the darkness, a man who loved to talk, trying desperately to be as quiet as a mouse. He could sense that his 13-year quest to bring major-league baseball to his city had never been closer to fulfillment. There could be no mistakes now. He would simply have to be patient in the dark until the president's son-in-law had had his say.

~ ~ ~

THE FIRST time I heard the voice of God, I was 19 years old.

Strangely, it came booming over the public-address system shortly before kickoff at Arlington High School's football stadium in the fall of 1965.

I hesitate to call it a religious experience. The earth didn't move, no nearby bushes burst into flame. It was a moment, however, that I would never forget.

Courtesy, Fort Worth Star-Telegram Collection, Special Collections, The University of Texas at Arlington Libraries

Tom Vandergriff throws out the first pitch before the Rangers' first game in Arlington in 1970, flanked by Rangers owner Bob Short, left, and American League President Joe Cronin, right.

I don't have to tell you that it's generally not normal for God to speak through the PA at a high school football game. Then again, "normal" was not the word anyone would choose to describe Tom Vandergriff.

So, no, not God ... but, in Arlington, Texas, pretty darn close.

I was in the press box that night because I had aced a spelling test in my interview and landed a job as the very young sports editor at the little *Arlington News Texan,* the city's only daily newspaper. I directed a staff of one — me. It was early September, and I was covering my first high school football game in my new hometown after moving from Carlsbad, N.M., following a semester at Texas Tech. My dad had a new job at General Motors.

I had heard good PA announcers before, but I had never heard a voice like the one I heard that night.

"Who is that?" I asked incredulously, looking around the press box. I was seriously thinking that, if God suddenly spoke from the heavens, this is how he would sound if he were welcoming everyone to a high school football Friday night.

"Oh, that's the mayor, Tom Vandergriff," someone said casually. "He announces all the high school games here and at Sam Houston, too."

I was impressed and intrigued. Since when does the mayor announce all of his town's high school football games? I would soon learn the answer: It's what you do when you can combine your love for your city and its people with your lifelong dream of being a broadcast journalist.

Tom Vandergriff was, is and will always be Mr. Arlington. General Motors, Six Flags, Lake Arlington, Arlington Memorial Hospital, UT-Arlington, the Texas Rangers and even the Dallas Cowboys (with a big nod to another mayor, Bob Cluck) — their existence in Arlington can be traced back to the passion and determination of one man.

There have been many heroes to celebrate in Texas Rangers lore — Nolan Ryan, Fergie Jenkins, Josh Hamilton, Jim Sundberg, Pudge Rodriguez, Juan Gonzalez — but only one deserves the honorary distinction of First Hero:

Tommy Joe Vandergriff.

There would be no Texas Rangers without Vandergriff. His story is well-known, but it should be told and retold so younger generations can understand that hard work, perseverance and undying passion *can* make the impossible dream a reality.

There were times when Vandergriff's 13-year quest to bring major-league baseball to the city once described as the hyphen between Dallas-Fort Worth had been derided as another Don-Quixote-tilting-at-windmills tale — but only by those who didn't really know the man known as "The Boy Mayor."

Vandergriff's tenacity in the face of heavy odds was established early. As a boy, he had stuttered horribly, and he spent years in speech therapy.

"I was determined to learn to talk and to talk well," Vandergriff would say later. "Within me was born the ambition to talk for a living."

When he graduated from the University of Southern California in 1947, he was intent on a career in broadcasting and applied for a job as a newscaster at a Los Angeles radio station.

The baritone-voiced Vandergriff felt sure the job would be his. There was, after all, just one other serious applicant.

"In fact, I did not think my competition was as good as me," Vandergriff would joke in retelling the story.

His competition — an unknown named Chet Huntley — got the job. That, of course, would be the Chet Huntley who would go on to national fame with David Brinkley on "The Huntley-Brinkley Report," which ran on NBC News from 1956 to 1970.

Crushed at the rejection, Vandergriff returned to the family automobile dealership business in Arlington in disappointment. Rather than pout, he threw himself into learning every nuance of the family car business. Politics and baseball, which would become his primary preoccupations over the next six decades, were the furthest things from his mind.

"I had no political aspirations at all, but I was interested in community endeavors," Vandergriff recalled. That desire to help the city grow prompted him to join the Arlington Chamber of Commerce. Just two years later, in 1949, he was elected its president. Two years after that, only 25, he was elected mayor of the about-to-explode small town nestled between the two giants to the east and west. It would be the first of 13 consecutive two-year terms.

"We had a small community," Vandergriff said, "but it was easy to see what could be done with this kind of geography at our fingertips."

A few months later, he found himself outside the office door of the chairman of General Motors in Detroit, waiting to sell the company on Arlington. GM wanted to build a plant in north Texas. Vandergriff knew what a catalyst a GM assembly line could be for his city.

The man who had struggled to speak clearly as a boy must have sounded good that day in the Motor City. Three years later, on Jan. 6, 1954, the first car rolled off the General Motors assembly line at the company's new Arlington plant on East Abram Street.

The GM plant in Arlington has been an economic engine for the region for going on 70 years now, generating tens of thousands of jobs and hundreds of millions of dollars for the local economy.

"I identified with the feeling that Arlington was a sleeping giant, and I had to be the city's salesman," Vandergriff said. "Even then there was the feeling that we needed a balanced community. Being an attractive bedroom residential suburb wasn't enough. We had to have industry. My first goal was to bring jobs to Arlington. I knew industry would be interested in locating in Arlington if they knew what we had to offer."

No city ever had a better promoter. "He could make a living selling beer to the Women's Christian Temperance Union," a *New York Times* reporter wrote after interviewing Vandergriff.

Vandergriff's family was another ace he had in the hole. When obstacles threatened to block a project Vandergriff deemed vital, it was the Vandergriff family itself that often rose to the occasion. When it became obvious that Arlington desperately needed its own hospital in 1957, the Vandergriff family donated 9 acres of land on the north side of town and spearheaded efforts to raise $250,000 for a 75-bed facility that would become Arlington Memorial Hospital.

By the time the story broke that General Motors was coming to Arlington, all but one landowner in the 225-acre plot targeted for the plant had signed an option to sell his property. The landowner held a lot in the heart of the site and used that as leverage to ask for more money. GM refused to raise its offer. Tom's father, Hooker Vandergriff, bought a premium piece of property on Abram and gave it to the landowner to help get the deal over the finish line.

GM was the first of dozens of major civic accomplishments by Vandergriff in his tireless zeal for Arlington. In 1958 he met with Walt Disney, hoping to persuade him to build a second Disneyland in Arlington. Developer Angus Wynne Jr. was offering Disney prime property for the project, but Disney was one of the few people to remain impervious to Vandergriff's passionate pitches. Undeterred, Vandergriff and Wynne decided to build their own amusement park in Arlington.

Six Flags Over Texas opened in August 1961. Today the Six Flags chain of theme parks that grew from that first Six Flags in Arlington is an internationally recognized brand.

Vandergriff's vision for Arlington was modeled in part on Anaheim, a Los Angeles suburb that had brought together an amusement park and a baseball team to become a tourist mecca. Six Flags would be the easier part of the formula. It would take 13 years for Vandergriff to land the prized jewel of his dream – a major-league baseball team.

If someone even hinted that a major-league team might be thinking of looking for greener pastures, Vandergriff was on a plane, pitching the little town that could. The Kansas City Athletics, the Cleveland Indians, the Cincinnati Reds, the Chicago White Sox, the Seattle Pilots, the San Diego Padres, the Pittsburgh Pirates — all considered, and eventually rejected, his pitch. In owners' offices and baseball's back rooms across the country, Vandergriff spent time wheeling, dealing, wrangling, prodding and pleading, but in the end no owner wanted to take a chance on a city many of them had never even heard of.

Finally, at the confluence of perseverance and desperation, came a breakthrough in the unlikeliest of places — the nation's capital, Washington, D.C. Unlikely because the president, one Richard M. Nixon, happened to be a baseball fan who abhorred any suggestion that might remove baseball from the nation's capital.

Bob Short was desperate, though. The Senators' owner had out-bid popular comedian Bob Hope to buy the expansion team for $9.4 million in 1968. Three years later, Short was realizing the joke was on him.

Attendance had peaked in 1969 at more than 900,000 during Ted Williams' first year as manager — the team's only winning season in the 11 years since it had arrived in D.C. as an expansion team after the original Senators elected to become the Minnesota Twins. Just two years later, the 1971 Senators lost 96 games, and attendance dropped by almost 300,000 fans.

The Senators seemed set on living up to the derisive description first coined by *Philadelphia Inquirer* baseball writer Charles Dryden in 1904: "Washington — First in war, first in peace, last in the American League."

Short, who couldn't scare up an offer in Washington, threatened that, if he couldn't get a local buyer for the team at $12.4 million, he would move it out of the city.

Baseball commissioner Bowie Kuhn and the politicians hooted at Short's threat. But guess who was listening intently and buying a ticket on the next plane bound for Washington, D.C.? Consider it a rhetorical question.

Vandergriff had come close to securing an MLB team for Arlington on several occasions, including Kansas City twice, before irascible Athletics owner Charlie Finley bolted at the altar. This time, though, Short and the Senators looked extremely promising to Vandergriff. That flight to Washington would be the first of so many that he could have applied for residency there.

His public pursuit of the Senators was so well-publicized, in fact, that he had practically become *persona non grata* in the nation's capital. On one trip a cab driver who discovered his passengers were from Texas asked if they by chance knew this insolent Texas mayor who was trying to steal the city's baseball team.

Vandergriff smiled pleasantly and admitted that indeed he did. In fact, he confessed, chuckling, he *was* that very mayor. The taxi driver instantly swung his cab to the curb and ordered Vandergriff and his 7-year-old daughter Viveca out of the vehicle.

It wasn't just die-hard Senators fans in the nation's capital who were ready to lynch Vandergriff. He found a variety of heavyweights lining up against him. He'd already gone head-to-head with Houston's Judge Roy Hofheinz, who considered the Dallas-Fort Worth area — and Texas in general — to be exclusive Astros territory. Hofheinz recruited LBJ to join the list of heavyweights opposing the move, including baseball commissioner Bowie Kuhn and President Nixon himself.

Despite the visit from Nixon's son-in-law that had occasioned the closet episode, though, Short proved amenable to what Vandergriff was offering.

Even after Vandergriff and Short had come to terms, there was one last hurdle: The final decision on the move would be made by the American League team owners.

Late in 1971, Vandergriff was invited to address the owners in a meeting in Boston. He would need the votes of 10 of the 12 owners for the move to be approved. Vandergriff counted several allies among them, the most supportive being the "Singing Cowboy" himself, Angels owner Gene Autry. But Autry was hospitalized and couldn't attend the meeting to support him, a development that didn't help Vandergriff's confidence.

A proxy had been sent to the hospital to secure Autry's "yea" vote. Vandergriff and his team still hoped Autry's vote might make the difference. Charlie Finley, who had twice come close to agreeing to move his Athletics to Arlington, had already tried a little arm-twisting, telling Vandergriff that he would vote for the move — but only if the Rangers sent young outfielder Jeff Burroughs to Kansas City. Vandergriff politely but firmly declined. If that meant Finley's vote was lost, so be it — even though the loss could torpedo Vandergriff's dream.

Commissioner Kuhn's opposition was well known, but another powerful voice would make one last dramatic pitch to keep the Senators in Washington. Amid the deliberations and debate, there was a knock at the door of the hotel conference room where the owners and the Texas contingent had gathered. American League president Joe Cronin ordered the door opened.

A porter solemnly walked into the silent room holding a silver plate upon which rested a single white envelope. The letter inside was addressed to the owners of the American League of Professional Baseball Clubs. Cronin read the letter silently, then announced that he would read it aloud to the entire assembly.

In a solemn voice, Cronin read: "I implore you. Repeat, I implore you. Do not move the nation's national pastime from the nation's capital."

It was signed "Richard M. Nixon, President of the United States of America."

The owners looked at each other and at Vandergriff.

Kuhn leaned over to young Texas lawyer Ray Hutchison, who was sitting beside him as part of Vandergriff's contingent. The commissioner dug an elbow into Hutchison's ribs and growled, "We've got you now, you sons of bitches!"

If it had been an NFL game, Kuhn would have been flagged for premature gloating with an extra 15 yards tacked on for unsportsmanlike conduct. There was little that Vandergriff, or the rest of the Texas contingent could say, though. They needed 10 owners to agree to the move, and how this unprecedented development might alter the vote was anyone's guess.

With the words of Nixon's plea still hanging in the air, Vandergriff was granted the final word — a closing argument.

Hutchison would later write of those excruciating moments in the *Dallas Morning News* after Vandergriff's passing in October of 2010: Vandergriff, he wrote, "made an extraordinary closing presentation and final plea. We were then dismissed from the room and called back about an hour and a half later. The (American League) president announced that, with only two dissents, the Washington Senators would move to Arlington, where they became the Texas Rangers."

Finley, it turned out, had relented and voted for the move. Only the Chicago White Sox and Baltimore Orioles owners had voted no, the former on the belief that moving baseball from the nation's capital would not be a good look for baseball and the latter out of concern that voting for the move might hurt their standing with fans in Washington, some of which supported both teams.

But Vandergriff didn't really care what their reasons were. He had secured his 10 votes. His 13-year quest to bring major-league baseball to his city was finally over.

~ ~ ~

BEFORE WE LEAVE the story, though, there's a little-known behind-the-scenes subplot that needs further illumination, and it's one that illustrates Tom Vandergriff's character.

Few remember — or perhaps ever knew — that the Vandergriff family came very close to *owning* the Rangers.

Remember, Short was in financial trouble. Vandergriff had offered several incentives to persuade him to move to Texas. One was a guarantee that a certain number of season tickets would be sold. The big one, though, was that Short would get the cash — $7.5 million — from the team's radio and TV rights up front.

That was big money in 1972, and the city was not involved in this part of the deal. Instead, Tom had turned to his dad, Hooker Vandergriff, for help. The elder Vandergriff pulled together a consortium of banks in Dallas to float the loan for Short, which Hooker then co-signed.

The elder Vandergriff added a caveat, insisting on a right of first refusal should Short ever decide to sell the team.

With the new Texas Rangers averaging less than 700,000 in the stands in each of their first two seasons, Short was ready to bail by 1974.

He went back to Hooker Vandergriff, as the contract stipulated, and asked if Hooker wanted to buy the team. Hooker had been biding his time, hoping this opportunity would come. He was ready to say yes. But Tom stepped in. He pleaded with his father not to go through with the purchase.

According to Tom Vandergriff's son Victor, Tom told his father, "You can't do it. If you buy the team now, then everything I've done at the city to get the Senators here is going to look like a game, just a private deal done for my own private interests."

Regretfully, Hooker Vandergriff told Short he was passing on the opportunity.

"He knew the optics would look bad," said Tom's grandson, Parker Vandergriff, the family historian. "He was afraid that people would think that all he'd done to bring the team here wasn't for the city but rather for our family."

Short would sell the team instead to Fort Worth plastic-pipe magnate Brad Corbett and a group of Dallas-Fort Worth investors.

A copy of the original contract resides in the Rangers archives, where current Rangers owner Ray Davis ran across it a few years ago. He was startled to discover that the Vandergriffs could have been the team's owners.

"He called me to ask about it," Parker Vandergriff said. "I told him the story, and he couldn't believe Hooker hadn't bought the team when he had the chance. He thought it was stupid. It's sort of a depressing joke in the family, how we could have owned the Rangers."

Not stupid at all, if you knew Tom Vandergriff. His integrity was never for sale at any price.

Still, imagine how different the Rangers' history might have been under a Vandergriff ownership dynasty much like the one Jerry Jones and his family have with the Cowboys.

What a dream story that would have been.

AT HALFTIME on that September night in 1965 at Arlington High, I had the opportunity to introduce myself to the owner of that voice over the P.A. I didn't know whether to kiss his ring or shake his hand. He was friendly, warm, gracious. He wasn't a deity after all. He was just Tom.

Those were the first moments of a friendship that would last until his death, some 45 years later. I was one of his biggest fans, and he became one of mine, dropping me the occasional hand-written note to praise a column in the *Star-Telegram* he had particularly enjoyed. Coming from him, I found those notes extremely encouraging.

After I penned a column about him upon his retirement as Tarrant County judge in late 2005, he graciously sent a note of thanks, which I still have and will always treasure. If you'll pardon the self-indulgence, it reads:

Dear Jim:
I am tardy in doing so but I must thank you for one of
the greatest kindnesses ever. That column of yours,

following my decision to retire from office was, without doubt, one of the most meaningful expressions I can recall relative to my efforts through the years. Please know of my heartfelt gratitude.

In return, allow me the privilege of stating that one of the best days ever for our region was when Jim Reeves cast his lot with us. There are times when I don't read every line in the Star-Telegram but I never fail to read each word in a Jim Reeves column.

Warm personal regards.

Sincerely,

Tom Vandergriff

I am as humbled and honored today by that personal note as I was when I received it more than 15 years ago.

There's a reason there's a statue of Tom Vandergriff outside Globe Life Field, only a few hundred yards from the very spot where the man once first established the Texas Rangers in Arlington. It stands there to remind us that a man of honor, of integrity, of vision, once dedicated his heart and soul to a mission that would bring millions the thrill and excitement of major-league baseball.

No, he wasn't God, of course. But that voice ... All these decades later, it still echoes in my mind.

Chapter 2

THE GIANT AMONG US
A Legend Comes to Texas: Ted Williams

*T*HE FIRST TEXAS RANGERS *team, in 1972, was a ragged mix of aging veterans with a sprinkling of young, mostly undeveloped talent. The one immediately recognizable figure, however, was the manager. If a Mt. Rushmore of Baseball were ever carved into the side of a mountain, his chiseled face would forever have a place there.*

TED WILLIAMS STOOD alone near the batting cage at Turnpike Stadium, legs slightly spread, arms folded across the front of his sky-blue Washington Senators warm-up jacket. Even in his mid-'50s he had an aura about him, a sense of barely contained power and charisma. It was as if John Wayne had swapped his six-shooter for a Louisville Slugger and was just waiting for some ne'er-do-well to wander into range.

The trick, I figured, was to make sure he didn't mistake me for said desperado.

That could be problematic. Ted's reputation as a fire-breathing, profanity-spouting ogre who devoured baseball writers as if polishing off a plate of hickory-smoked brisket was well-established. Therefore, the small cadre of newspaper and radio reporters who had assembled in the spring of 1971 at Turnpike Stadium, minor-league home of the Dallas-Fort Worth Spurs, clustered timidly in front of the first-base dugout, out of dining range. None of us relished the idea of being Ted's next appetizer.

The Senators were in town to play the Montreal Expos, the second half of a two-day major-league exhibition series that had also brought the Baltimore Orioles to Arlington. A day earlier, awestruck by my first encounter with big-league ballplayers, I had interviewed Orioles first baseman Boog Powell, who seemed to me gargantuan. When I commented on his size, Boog laughed, which from my vantage point was akin to being at the epicenter of an earthquake.

"Wait till the Senators get here tomorrow and you get a load of Hondo," he bellowed. "Now that is a *really* big man."

Powell was talking about the Senators' colossal first baseman and outfielder Frank Howard (who a little more than a year later would hit the Texas Rangers' first-ever home run). Howard was indeed massive: 6-foot-7 and 260 pounds of pure muscle. He brought to mind Jimmy Dean's classic hit "Big Bad John."

Howard towered over everyone in sight. Even so, we all knew who the real giant on the field was. By legend, myth and the record book, Ted Williams dwarfed everyone.

For those of us in the pen-and-notebook crowd, he also appeared to be licking his chops, silently enjoying the reporters' predicament. Would any of us have the nerve to approach the man who was so legendary he even had two nicknames: "The Splendid Splinter" and "The Kid"?

The three major local newspapers largely sent out their second-string — or, in my case, end-of-the-bench — sports reporters for these exhibition games. After all, this wasn't the Dallas Cowboys we were talking about. Most of us were young, inexperienced, terrified. None of us wanted to be the first to risk public humiliation from the great "Teddy Ballgame." (Oops! Did I say *two* nicknames?)

Someone, though, had to make the first move, or the lot of us would have stood there trembling like sheep on shearing day until the ump declared, "Play ball!"

I did have a strategy, of sorts. I haltingly edged the few yards from our collective post near the dugout toward the batting cage where Williams stood. As soon as I was within earshot, I started babbling ...

... about fishing.

Everyone knew how much Ted Williams loved to fish and hunt. I figured this off-the-wall ploy had a chance to be the safest icebreaker possible. If things went south, maybe he would only maim me, not gut me on the spot like a freshly caught Florida bonefish.

Guess what? It worked.

Williams immediately started asking questions about the fishing and hunting in North Texas. What were the best lakes close by? What kind of fish were the fishermen going after? Were coyotes fair game for hunters? Rifle or shotgun? Any good spots for fly fishing? Sure, he sprinkled in an amazing assortment of four-letter epithets, but at least he wasn't aiming them in my direction.

Seeing that I hadn't been eviscerated, the other reporters gradually began to drift over. The conversation segued easily to baseball. Of course, not one of my lily-livered journalistic brethren troubled themselves to say thank you for my incredible display of fortitude and courage.

~ ~ ~

THIS WAS MY introduction to Ted Williams, arguably the greatest purveyor of lumber against horsehide who ever lived. Certainly that's what *he* would tell you — and basically did, in his book "The Science of Hitting." In any case, I sure as hell wasn't going to argue with him.

As things developed, a year later Ted would reluctantly return to Texas — as the manager of the newly transplanted and rechristened version of the Washington Senators, now known as the Texas Rangers. Washington, a long-ago baseball writer had declared, had been "first in war, first in peace, last in the American League." The new Rangers' motto in Arlington was much simpler: First in line at Gaylen's Bar-B-Q.

Arlington Mayor Tom Vandergriff's impossible dream had come true. Major League Baseball had arrived to stay in North Texas. If the ragged nature of the stadium, players and team belied that statement, at least the manager didn't.

They don't get any bigger than Ted Williams.

That Ted would remain only the one year wasn't because he didn't favor Texas and the quality of its black-bass fishing; he just didn't much enjoy managing any more. Not surprisingly, burnout had begun to set in.

After three years at Washington's helm, including the team's only winning season in its 11-year history (1969), he had reluctantly come to understand that he would never be able to impart what he had hoped to teach his players about hitting. It wasn't because they didn't try. They simply couldn't do what had always come so easily to Teddy Ballgame.

Texas Rangers manager Ted Williams, with players wearing cowboy hats, on opening night on April 21, 1972, in Arlington.

"I would hear him say, 'In the early part of the game I would try to hit the top of the baseball, for line drives, drives to the gaps,'" Rich Billings, starting catcher on that first Rangers team, recalled later. "Then he'd say, 'Later in the game I would try to elevate the baseball for home runs.' I think he thought the rest of us mortals should do the same.

"Are you kidding me? Nolan Ryan is throwing a hundred miles an hour, then throwing a curveball that starts behind my back and breaks on the outside part of the plate, and I'm supposed to be thinking about which half of the baseball I'm going to hit?

"People like that just seem to take their ability for granted and can't relate to the average or below-average player like me. We just didn't have the talent he did. We couldn't hit the top half of the baseball or the bottom half of the baseball; we were just hoping to hit any part of the damn ball."

Billings and future Rangers general manager Tom Grieve, then a young Senators-Rangers outfielder, loved to listen to Williams talk hitting, but Ted's overwhelming force of personality often made it uncomfortable, too.

"Ted was like a split personality," Billings said. "I've never seen anyone who could hold an audience [as well], with people listening to every word he said, whether it was about hitting, fishing, cameras.

He knew more about hitting than anyone I'd ever been around, period. But he could be so cantankerous and argumentative in a baseball uniform, it was sometimes hard to be around him.

"Out of uniform he had a normal, ordinary persona."

Billings has never forgotten one of the most uncomfortable moments with his Hall of Fame manager, in Baltimore in '71. Williams was lounging in the corner of the dugout holding court with a covey of local baseball writers and columnists when Billings ambled out of the tunnel and turned to the bat rack, searching for some lumber for batting practice. Williams, playing to his audience, leaned over and poked his catcher in the back with a fungo bat.

"Look at this big dummy," Williams wisecracked to the reporters with their pens poised over notepads. "I doubt he has ever read my book."

Billings, embarrassed but determined to keep things light, turned with a smile.

"As a matter of fact, I did read your book," Billings retorted. "But if I read a medical journal, it still wouldn't make me a doctor."

It was a funny line, just what the eager writers were looking for. They hooted and scribbled away. Williams, though, was embarrassed and furious at being one-upped. Moments later he went after Billings, poked him in the chest and ordered him, as Billings recalls, to "get my blankety-blank ass to the bullpen and don't come back until I tell you."

The team's starting catcher and clean-up hitter, Billings spent the next three games in the bullpen warming up relievers. More than half a century later, the memory still stings.

"What I was trying to say," Billings sighed over the phone from his home in Michigan, "was that I could read your book all day long and not hit like you."

Billings had a point. Many people read the book, but no one else ever hit like the Kid.

Grieve, who had been the Senators' first-round draft pick (sixth overall) in 1966, had similar feelings.

"It was obvious to most of us that Ted didn't really enjoy being a big-league manager," Grieve said. "But if you asked him a question about hitting, you better get a cup of coffee and sit down."

With the possible exception of Joe DiMaggio, no one prided him-

Courtesy, Fort Worth Star-Telegram Collection, Special Collections, The University of Texas at Arlington Libraries

Ted Williams with his cowboy boots on opening night at Arlington Stadium in 1972.

self on his accomplishments in the game more than Williams.

"Once Rich [Billings] hit a ball into the upper deck at Comiskey Park during batting practice, and we're all oohing and aahing around the batting cage," Grieve said. "Ted pointed to a seat way up in center-field and said, 'Hit one up there, then brag.'"

It was where Ted himself had once launched a 500 plus-foot home run.

"How could you not say you wanted to be on the same team as Ted Williams?" Grieve said. "He was just frustrated by the fact that he couldn't turn so many of us average players into the kind of player he thought he should be able to talk us into being.

"You read his book, you understand he wanted you to swing with a slight uppercut, to be patient. The problem was we just weren't as talented as he was."

Grieve thought back to when the Rangers were playing the Red Sox in Fenway Park in '72 in one of the annual Jimmy Fund games supporting cancer research. It had been Ted's favorite charity since he broke in with the Bosox back in 1939. The Sox had invited a dozen or so retired players to put on an exhibition during batting practice, and Williams was one of them. Many of the old-time Red Sox sluggers were there, Grieve recalled, Fenway heroes like Dick Gernert, Walt

Dropo, Jackie Jensen. They all took their swings.

"You knew Ted would be the last hitter," Grieve said. "Sitting in the dugout, you could hear him clattering down the wooden walkway in the tunnel from the clubhouse. He walked out into the dugout with such focus in his eyes. He didn't know or care whether anyone else was in the dugout or in the stands.

"He rummaged through the bat rack, cussing this bat and that, then he started swearing at the pine-tar rag because it was too greasy, not sticky enough. He picked up a resin bag and some dirt and finally got it the way he wanted it, then came the announcement everyone was waiting for: 'Baseball's greatest living hitter, Ted Williams!'"

Williams leapt out of the dugout, bat in one hand, ripping his jacket off with the other and screaming at batting-practice pitcher Lee Stange, "Don't throw that soft shit to me! Put something on it!"

Just as he had in practically every at-bat in his illustrious career, Williams took the first pitch. Then he proceeded to rocket 12 or 15 line drives into the Fenway outfield. Red Sox fans screamed uncontrollably. Some swooned on the spot. In the press box, the clatter of typewriters recording the moment for posterity was deafening. "Stop the presses!" someone screamed. It was that kind of moment.

Dramatically, "The Splendid Splinter" threw down his bat, waved at the roaring and adoring fans (something he rarely did when he was playing) and vanished back into the clubhouse.

Classic Ted Williams.

Grieve, wide-eyed, turned to Rangers first-base coach Nellie Fox sitting alongside him on the bench.

"That was amazing," Grieve said. "He probably hasn't taken batting practice in years, and he comes out here and hits like that!"

Fox, cheek bulging with his perpetual plug of chewing tobacco, shook his head ruefully and grinned.

"What do you mean? He's been taking batting practice under the stands [in Arlington] for six weeks knowing this was coming. You think Ted would come in here and do something like this and not be prepared?"

WILLIAMS' HITTING prowess was matched by his status as a world-class, Olympics-level dispenser of profanity. In a sport where the four-letter word is king, he was by all accounts unmatched in his ability to produce new and innovative ways to say the most vulgar things, no matter who happened to be nearby.

"No one ever strung profanities together like he did," Grieve declared in admiration. "One of the classics was hearing Ted and George Susce, our bullpen coach, get into an argument about who had the best hot-fudge sundaes, Howard Johnson's or this little place back in Boston called Friendly's. Here they are, talking about hot-fudge sundaes and using every foul word you can think of, and some you would never think of. It was absolutely hilarious."

On another occasion, 14-year-old batboy Victor Vandergriff, son of Arlington mayor and local saint Tom Vandergriff, found himself innocently awash in Ted's XXX-rated verbiage.

"Ted had a perch built in the corner of the dugout, so he didn't have to stand up to look out," Grieve said. "During one game he went off on this incredible run of profanities with religious overtones. I look over, and poor Victor's hunkered down beside Ted. He had this look on his face like he'd seen a ghost. He was afraid to move, afraid to stand up.

"Frankly, I didn't blame him. I pretty much felt the same way."

Anyone and anything were fair game for Williams' profane outbursts. During that first Rangers season, outfielder Ted Ford slid into second base during a game in Kansas City and injured his knee. Texas trainer Bill Zeigler, who was such a Ted Williams fan he'd named his eldest son Ted Williams Zeigler, consulted with the Royals' team doctor. They decided Ford needed a trip to the emergency room. When Zeigler walked into Williams' office to tell the manager of the plan, he found Williams' boss Bob Short there, embroiled in a tense argument with Williams.

Short, perpetually short on money, wasn't thrilled with Zeigler's decision to transport Ford to an ER. He told Zeigler that, if he couldn't do his job — which, in this case, would appear to have meant miraculously healing Ford — Short would find a trainer who could. Williams immediately turned on Short with such prolific and profane virulence that Zeigler was awestruck.

"Ted's language," Zeigler would later say in hushed tones, "was indescribable."

Some of Zeigler's favorite times were on the road when Williams would arrive at the ballpark early, which was rare, and head to the dugout. In Minneapolis, Harmon Killebrew would often drift over to talk hitting. In Detroit, it might be Al Kaline.

"I was like a fly on the wall, trying to soak it all in, listening to these great players talk hitting," Zeigler said. Then again, Zeigler was such a fan that he felt much the same sense of awe just watching Williams eat a peanut-butter sandwich in his underwear.

~ ~ ~

BACK IN Arlington, Williams' favorite post-game hangout was Gaylen's Bar-B-Q, conveniently situated not much more than a home run's distance west of Arlington Stadium on North Collins Street. Gaylen's was a favorite of those locals who preferred their barley and hops with a thin skim of ice on top and their brisket hot and juicy.

Ted enjoyed the convenience, the brisket and especially the ambience. The walls at Gaylen's were covered with lunker bass and hunting trophies owner Gaylen Gilbreath had personally hooked or shot over the years. An oversized aquarium frequently sported a recently caught lunker bass or two swimming around.

The place was often closed by the time Ted arrived, but Gilbreath would obligingly unlock the door and allow Williams in. He'd load the table with platters of hickory-smoked brisket and ribs and icy mugs of draft beer. Then they would talk fishing and hunting for a couple of hours. Rumor has it they might have dropped a few lures into the aquarium now and then as well.

The bass never had a chance, and there's a better-than-zero chance that Galbreath also heard a little about the art of hitting.

Williams would essentially be gone from baseball after that single season in Texas. What he'd meant to the game as a player simply could not be duplicated as a manager. The genius Ted Williams brought to hitting, augmented by his incredible reflexes, his vision, his strength, was not something that could be passed on to others.

With a bat in his hands, Ted Williams was a god. With a lineup card, he was, unfortunately, a mere mortal, dependent on the talents of others. What should never be forgotten, however, is that he was instrumental in helping a small band of intrepid adventurers gain a toehold in north Texas.

Even when the Rangers were losing 100 games in 1972, when they didn't have a single player who could remotely be called a star, they still had the one and only Ted Williams.

Fifty years ago, you see, a giant lived among us.

Chapter 3

THE SACRIFICIAL SAVIOR
David Clyde, the Golden Boy

*I*N 1973, TEXAS RANGERS *baseball was foundering. The team had lost 100 games in '72 and was on its way to another 105 for the season. Owner Bob Short was out of money and patience. He needed a miracle — or the franchise might well collapse into bankruptcy or a takeover by the American League.*

Then, in June of 1973, an 18-year-old "angel," fresh from the high school fields of Tomball, Texas, pulled on a Rangers uniform and performed CPR on the gasping franchise. Many believed he saved major-league baseball in north Texas. If so, it came at a steep price: his enormously promising career.

Courtesy, Fort Worth Star-Telegram Collection, Special Collections, The University of Texas at Arlington Libraries

David Clyde awaits his major-league debut against the Minnesota Twins.

ALMOST 50 YEARS LATER, David Clyde's most vivid recollection of that day is 15 minutes of pure, excruciating agony.

They would be the last 15 minutes of life as he had known it, the last 900 seconds before the 18-year-old would step onto the mound at Arlington Stadium and make his first professional pitch.

They ticked by, one by one, like cold molasses inching in thick brown globs from an upended jar.

Plop … plop … plop …

When they were gone, nothing would ever be the same again.

"It's still surreal to this day," Clyde, 66, recalled from his home in Humble, Texas, just 35 minutes northwest of the town of Tomball, where he was living when he became arguably the most famous high school pitcher in baseball history.

"When was the last time a major-league baseball game was delayed to allow the crowd to get in?" Clyde asked.

Better question: When was the last time an 18-year-old high-school grad made his major-league baseball debut less than three weeks after pitching in the state high school baseball tournament?

Easy: June 27, 1973. Maybe you were there; just about every baseball fan in north Texas claims to have been in the crowd.

Joe Cronin, the American League president at the time, called it baseball's biggest debut "since Bob Feller came out of Iowa." (In case you don't remember that one, it was a pretty big deal, too.)

As spectacles go, what happened on that day nearly half a century ago in Arlington, Texas, population 90,000, hasn't been seen in major-league baseball again and likely never will be.

As melodramas go, it was nothing less than a heartbreaking American tragedy, with an 18-year-old in the role of both hero and victim.

~ ~ ~

IT HAD ALL begun three weeks earlier, on June 5, 1973, when the Texas Rangers selected 18-year-old David Eugene Clyde of Tomball, Texas, with the first overall pick of baseball's annual first-year draft.

A glance today at that '73 draft list shows that it was littered with future Hall of Famers and notable players. No one, however, was surprised when David Clyde's name was the first one called out by MLB Commissioner Bowie Kuhn.

The young southpaw had scouts and managers all over baseball foaming at the mouth. At Houston's Westchester High School, he had just wrapped up one of the most amazing seasons in the history of high school baseball. He'd gone 18-0 with an 0.18 ERA, 328 strikeouts in 148 innings and five no-hitters, two of them perfect games. He had thrown 14 complete game shutouts and set 14 national records, some of which still stand.

Some were comparing the youngster to Sandy Koufax, arguably

the greatest left-hander baseball had ever seen. The kid had even picked Rangers jersey number 32, the same number Koufax wore. It wasn't a coincidence. Drafting and signing Clyde was considered a huge coup for the Rangers. If all the aforementioned hype hadn't been enough to stir up a fan frenzy, the fact that this prodigy hailed from Texas was a bonus — catnip to the Rangers' fans.

As my former *Fort Worth Star-Telegram* colleague Mike Shropshire wrote in his hilarious book *Seasons in Hell,* manager Whitey Herzog had things all planned out for Clyde before the Rangers signed him. They would get him some fine-tuning in the rookie league, where he could be around teammates his own age and become accustomed to being away from home. Once the kid had developed a change-up to go along with his fastball and curve, he'd be bumped up to Double or Triple A. By the time he was 20, he'd be ready for the big leagues.

"And after that," joked Herzog, who had just watched Secretariat win the Belmont Stakes by 30 lengths, "we can bottle his sperm."

It was a fine plan, but you know what they say; managers make plans, and the baseball gods roll in the floor laughing. Wouldn't it be a show, the increasingly desperate Short thought, if the Rangers brought Clyde straight out of high school to the major leagues? How many tickets might they sell?

Just one game, Short thought. Just one.

The Clydes — David's dad Gene was handling his son's negotiations — hadn't asked for a ticket straight to the majors, but they didn't flinch at the idea either. What 18-year-old would?

"What was I supposed to do? Ask to be sent to the minor leagues?" Clyde said.

Privately Herzog was telling Randy Galloway and the other beat writers that this was a bad idea. But he also knew Short was trying to attract potential buyers. The owner needed something to call attention to the franchise, a selling point. Herzog had no choice but to go along with the owner and hope the Tomball kid could handle the pressure.

The announcement ignited baseball fans like nothing ever had in the franchise's brief history in Texas. It was like a rolling prairie fire, spreading not just throughout the state, but across the country as well. Perhaps it was the audacity of the idea, starting an 18-year-old straight out of high school in the majors. Certainly part of the allure

Eighteen-year-old David Clyde was selected with the first overall pick of baseball's annual first-year draft in 1973.

was Clyde's incredible high school numbers and the scouts' comparisons to Koufax.

The Rangers' decision merited mention on national TV broadcasts and in the *New York Times*. Ticket sales were going through the roof, and the Rangers' tiny public-relations office was besieged by credential requests for coverage. On the day of the game, someone counted at least two dozen TV crews from stations all over Texas.

THE RANGERS did what they could to prepare Clyde and themselves for the uproar that followed his selection and the club's unprecedented decision to pitch him three weeks later.

This was a team that was averaging barely more than 8,300 for home games. Only three times in the season's first 66 games had the Rangers drawn more than 20,000 fans. Suddenly, with the announcement of the wunderkind's pitching debut, the ticket office was overwhelmed with excited customers.

On Monday, two days before Clyde would be pitching against star contact hitter Rod Carew and the Twins, advance sales had already eclipsed the franchise record of 24,222, set on a July promotion night the previous season. Another 6,500 tickets were sold that day, leaving only 8,000 remaining in the converted minor-league ballpark. Every one of them would be snatched up the following day.

Clyde made his first appearance in a Texas uniform that Monday night against Oakland, when Herzog sent him to the plate with the lineup card. He hadn't even been out of high school for three weeks yet. The handsome teen-ager casually sauntered out to join A's manager Dick Williams. He introduced himself to the umpires, who broke into grins. With his curly brown hair, dark-eyed good looks and ear-to-ear smile, Clyde was an instant hit with the fans.

"Well, I thought I'd give the fans a look at David, and — hell, did you see how the kid handled himself?" Herzog told reporters. "Just like a major-leaguer."

"You really think the kid is ready for this?" someone asked.

"It's a lot of pressure for a kid," Herzog conceded, "but if there's any 18-year-old in the country who can handle it, David would be it. This is a super kid with a good head on his shoulders."

Indeed, Clyde seemed incredibly poised. He was articulate, thoughtful, unflappable, hardly your average stammering, pimply-faced teen-ager. When someone told him that some 28,000 tickets had already been sold, Clyde shrugged.

"That many, huh? Well, I don't have anything against big crowds. That many is fine with me.

"What I'd like to do is ignore the crowd altogether and just concentrate on trying to hit the target, you know, just throw strikes. But I'm sure if this place is full of people, I'll notice. If anything, it will pump me up. Already I can feel the adrenaline pumping.

"I'm getting excited now. I'm starting to think about it more and more. The butterflies won't start until Tuesday night, but tonight I can feel them coming. I know it means a lot of pressure, the big crowd and everything. But I've always pitched well under pressure. I like to think that under pressure is when I'm at my best."

Besides, he said, he'd pitched before big crowds before.

"In high school I've pitched before 7,000 on two different occasions, and you can imagine at a high school field how crowded and loud that was."

For the first time, he sounded a bit naïve.

The day before Clyde's debut, which had captured not just the fancy of Texans from El Paso to Texarkana but the attention of the entire baseball-loving nation, *Dallas Morning News* Rangers beat writer Randy Galloway sounded a prophetic note of caution in a column.

"What the Rangers are asking of Clyde possibly smacks of exploitation, a seamy work which can have all sorts of ramifications," Galloway wrote. "There are those who say it's unfair to ask so much from one so young, particularly one without professional experience. But then, this is the opportunity Clyde wanted, an opportunity his father [Gene], who negotiated for him, felt he should have, and one [owner Bob] Short was more than happy to oblige him with."

Fending off the critics, Herzog sounded a bit like a man who's about to eat oysters for the first time trying to convince himself they can't really taste as bad as they look.

"This isn't some kind of gimmick," Herzog insisted a little irritably. "We're not throwing that kid out there just to create interest. We've sold a lot of tickets because of him, but then David Clyde is the type of pitcher who can sell a hell of a lot more tickets before he's through. If we didn't think he was major-league caliber, and if everyone in baseball didn't think he was major-league caliber, we wouldn't be pitching him.

"I had six or seven general managers come up to me saying the kid is ready for the big leagues right now. Our scouts are saying the same thing."

Maybe young David *was* ready for that day, ready to slay the Goliaths of major-league baseball. He just wasn't ready for what came after.

～ ～ ～

ON WEDNESDAY, the day of Clyde's much-anticipated debut, the entire Rangers organization reported for duty as if going to war. Extra ticket-takers were dispatched to the front lines. Additional concession workers and parking-lot attendants were standing by. Platoons of beer vendors began stocking their coolers.

Clyde slept in, then breakfasted at his hotel around noon as TV cameras captured every forkful of his scrambled eggs, every nibble of bacon. Afterward, he ushered his three younger brothers over to the stadium and into the Rangers clubhouse for a quick visit before retreating to his hotel to rest up for the night's show.

A telegram arrived. It read: *"Good luck No. 32; go get 'em."* It was signed *Sandy Koufax.*

By 5:30 p.m., Clyde was at the stadium, changing into his baseball uniform, jersey No. 32.

Nerves began an assault on his stomach within minutes, sending him scurrying to a bathroom stall. He emerged pale but smiling and finished dressing.

"Nervous?" veteran catcher Rich Billings incredulously echoed a questioner. "Hell, yes, he's nervous. I'm nervous, and I'm not even playing."

In the first-base dugout, Herzog said he'd suggested Clyde drink a beer to settle himself down. He was joking, trying to keep the mood light. The manager conceded to reporters hanging on his every word that his only regret, now that the big day has arrived, was not pitching Clyde for a couple of innings Sunday in Kansas City. Maybe then, he reasoned, the kid would have gotten the first-game jitters out of the way in a less pressurized atmosphere. But he quickly brushed away his own second-guessing.

"I promised our fans they would see him first, and they haven't had a lot to cheer about, so I wanted to keep that promise," he said.

In the stands, Clyde's parents, brothers, grandparents and a great aunt and uncle settled into their seats. They were quickly joined by David's girlfriend Cheryl Crawford and her parents.

Cheryl was wearing a red-and-white hot-pants outfit (this was 1973, remember) that matched her boyfriend's brand-new $6,500 Buick Electra, as well as a "promise ring" she enjoyed showing off to the photographers clustered around her. She seemed bemused by the attention David was drawing from other young women in the crowd.

"I'm just glad to see that other women find him attractive," she told reporters, a statement she may have regretted later. (The high-school sweethearts would be married within months and divorced a little more than a year after that.)

Clyde's high school coach Bob French was also in the stands, as was Peter Ramirez, his Little League coach from Topeka, Kansas, the state where Clyde spent much of his childhood. Ramirez said he had a class the next day and planned on boarding a bus back to Kansas immediately after the game. It'd be worth the long trip, he said, to see David pitch in the big leagues.

On the field, all that was missing was a calliope and dancing elephants. There was a ringmaster, though: Bob Short was everywhere, beaming in white sports coat and blue slacks.

Being neighborly, Arlington's two theme parks, Six Flags and Seven Seas, had sent over a troupe of giant papier-mâché animals. There were real lion cubs from Lion Country Safari down the road in Grand Prairie. Hula dancers were gyrating everywhere. Kids were running helter-skelter through the stands, so excited they were even asking ushers for their autographs.

Forty-five minutes before game time, Clyde joined Herzog in the dugout, wide-eyed at the hoopla on the field. Herzog, playing into the Bob Short hype machine, allowed reporters to linger in the dugout longer than usual. They chronicled Clyde's every blink, every twitch, every scratch.

Clyde sat, nervously tapping his knee to the music over the P.A. "I can't wait to get under way," he said softly. "I can't wait to get under way."

Herzog sat down beside him, draping an arm over his shoulders. "OK, I want you to do everything tonight but throw." Clyde laughed.

Starting catcher Ken Suarez was sitting close by.

"Ken, I want you to chew his tail out if he needs it," Herzog said with mock seriousness.

Suarez blinked.

"Hell," Suarez said, "I'll probably say, 'Yessir.'"

Pitching coach Chuck Estrada walked by, registered mock surprise and asked Clyde, "What are you doing out here?"

Next came shortstop Toby Harrah. He reached over and turned Clyde's cap backward, saying, "That adds some class." A photographer urged Clyde to keep it that way, but he hurriedly turned it back around.

Pulling a baseball out of his pocket, Herzog held it out for Clyde to see. "OK, kid, this is a baseball," Herzog said. Again, everyone chuckled. The tension built like afternoon storm clouds.

Meanwhile, the boisterous sellout crowd, which eventually would grow to 35,698, continued to pour in as game time approached.

It was becoming obvious that not everyone would be in their seats for the first pitch. Cars were lined up for miles both east and west on the Dallas-Fort Worth Turnpike bordering the Arlington Stadium parking lot. Late-arriving fans were pushing toward the gates, threatening to overwhelm ticket-takers. For the first time in the Rangers' brief history, scalpers were doing a brisk business outside the gates. Ticket manager Joe Sullivan would say later that he could have sold another 10,000 tickets if he had had the seats.

As Clyde began his slow stroll to the bullpen down the rightfield line to begin his warmup routine, Herzog was conferring by phone with general manager Joe Burke. Burke informed him about the traffic jam on the turnpike, the crowd at the gates. Whitey was concerned that too many fans would still be outside when Clyde took the mound. They agreed to push the first pitch back 15 minutes.

The news was relayed to Clyde through the bullpen phone just as he was about to start stretching before his first warmup pitch. Sit down, Herzog advised him.

Clyde was devastated.

Almost 50 years later, he still recalled how hearing those words — *15-minute delay* — hit him like someone plunging a knife into his guts and twisting.

"It felt like I was 10 years old again and someone was telling me that it's not Christmas Day after all," he told me for this book. "I couldn't wait for the game. The game, the field, was the only place where I felt normal. It was the only sane place for me on the face of the planet that day.

"I was so ready to get it over with, to finally get started. Are you kidding me? It was the longest 15 minutes of my life. That's what I remember most about that day."

Fueled by the adrenaline spilling into his bloodstream, Clyde was a bundle of jangling nerves when he finally took the mound against the Twins. His first pitch to Twins leadoff hitter Jerry Terrell, a fastball, was low — a ball. He threw a strike, then two more balls. On the 3-1 count, he missed low again.

Next up was Rod Carew, coming off the first of four straight American League batting titles. Carew walked on four straight pitches out of the strike zone. The crowd stirred uneasily.

Two on, nobody out. Clyde had thrown nine pitches, and eight had been balls.

"I thought, 'Good Lord, it's going to be a long first inning. I'm not going to get anybody out, and they're going to start ripping me,'" Clyde would say after the game.

Clyde started power hitter Bobby Darwin with a fastball, too far inside. Then David pumped fastball, curveball, fastball — all strikes — and Darwin was out. The crowd leapt to its feet with a standing ovation.

Cleanup hitter George Mitterwald went down swinging. When first baseman Joe Lis did the same, the crowd was back on its feet, roaring. *The kid had fanned the side!* There was delirium in the stands.

~ ~ ~

THE AFTERMATH ...

Clyde would go on to throw 121 pitches in five innings, allowing the Twins just one hit, a two-run home run to leftfielder Mike Adams in the second inning. Walking seven and striking out eight, he left the mound with a 4-2 lead. Bill Gogolewski went the final four innings, securing a 4-3 win. Herzog was so pleased with Gogo he told him he didn't even have to come to the ballpark the next day.

"From now on," Arlington Mayor Tom Vandergriff proclaimed solemnly after the game, "time here shall be marked from June 27, 1973."

In the visiting clubhouse, the Twins were mostly complimentary about the Texas teenager. Rod Carew, though, had a blunt assessment.

"You want to hear the truth, right? I wasn't all that impressed," Carew told reporters. "His fastball isn't that exceptional, and he doesn't have a good breaking ball. He's no (Vida) Blue. We were chasing pitches we shouldn't have."

The *Morning News'* headline the next morning referenced a couple of shady Texas legends: "A Bonnie Debut for Clyde."

After Clyde's successful debut, the plan for him changed yet again. Now Herzog was saying that maybe the Rangers would keep Clyde around for a couple of starts, then send him to the lower minors to learn how to be a professional.

There was also talk of shutting him down completely for the rest of the season to protect his still-developing arm. After all, he had already thrown almost 150 innings in high school.

Once Short saw the boost Clyde was giving his bottom line, though, there was no way he was sending his meal ticket to the boonies. The day before Clyde made his debut, the Rangers had drawn 6,238 fans. The day after, it was 3,992. Through July, whenever Clyde started, the Rangers' average attendance was 25,844. When anyone else started, it plummeted to 7,000 or so.

Besides that, Clyde was pitching well. In his second start against the White Sox, he gave up just a single earned run in six innings. On the road for the first time in Milwaukee, he struggled a bit but bounced back with an exceptional performance at Boston.

A banner headline in the *Boston Globe* the morning of his fourth start read: "Kid Sensation to Face Sox Tonight at Fenway."

Not in the sports section, mind you, but on the front page.

The normally hostile Boston crowd, having been known to eviscerate visiting rookies, stood and politely applauded as Clyde ambled from the dugout to the bullpen beyond the right-field fence to warm up. He pitched gamely, holding the Sox to seven hits and two runs in six innings. He walked none, struck out eight and left trailing 2-1 in a game the Rangers eventually lost, 5-2.

If Carew hadn't been all that impressed, the Red Sox certainly were.

"In my second at-bat, the kid threw as well as any pitcher I have faced in my career," said future Hall of Famer Carl Yastrzemski. "The ball seemed to come out of nowhere. He struck me out, and I wasn't surprised when he did."

Orlando Cepeda compared Clyde favorably to Koufax, "and that means trouble for the hitters in this league."

Luis Aparicio, on the tail-end of a career that would land him in Cooperstown, said, "I've never been so impressed with a young pitcher."

By the middle of August, Clyde was 4-4 with 3.21 ERA on a team headed for 105 losses. Then the bottom dropped out, and all the evidence points to sheer overuse. Over his next five starts, Clyde averaged less than three innings per outing. He was cooked.

No sense mincing words this far down the road, and it's not as though they haven't been written many times before: David Clyde was owner Bob Short's sacrificial lamb, trussed up, laid on the altar of the pitching mound and bled until he had no more to give.

There were those who said the sacrifice was necessary to save baseball in north Texas, given the team's dire circumstances leading up to the season. In the direct aftermath, when the brief and troubled career of David Clyde as a major-league pitcher had died its premature death, that seemed as good a narrative as any. The rationale provided an alibi of sorts for Short and the others who allowed a young man's dream to be shattered like the shards of a mirror.

Fifty years of hindsight, research and reflection allows a different perspective:

What a crock.

~ ~ ~

THAT "SAVIOR of baseball" narrative has been an easy storyline for sports feature writers, me included, for half a century. But the hard truth is that what happened to Clyde was never about saving baseball in Arlington.

The Clyde debacle was always about saving Short's financial skin — nothing more, nothing less. If hindsight tells us anything, the idea that Major League Baseball would have given up on the Dallas-Fort Worth area just two years after Short moved the team from Washington, D.C., to Arlington is ludicrous.

And does anyone seriously think that Tom Vandergriff, after a decades-long quest that included going head-to-head with the president of the United States, was going to allow Arlington's team to slip away?

Not a chance, and here's the tell: As mentioned in an earlier chapter, when current Rangers owner Ray Davis found the original contract detailing Short's eventual sale of the Rangers to Brad Corbett in 1974, his attention was caught by an interesting clause: Hooker Vandergriff, Tom's father, had held the right of first refusal if Short ever decided to sell the team.

The elder Vandergriff had fully intended to buy the Rangers himself, until Tom intervened and begged his father not to exercise the clause. He was afraid that all the work he'd done for the city of Arlington to bring the Senators to Texas would appear to have been for the benefit of the Vandergriff family.

On the other hand, if Tom had needed Hooker to step in to keep the Rangers from leaving town … I have a feeling he might have had a change of heart, as distasteful as he might have found it.

Always follow the money: The whole idea behind the move from Washington for Short was to find a wealthy Texan on whom he might unload his moribund franchise. The Minnesota trucking/real-estate/hotel magnate wanted out of the sports franchise business. Remember, he'd bought the Minneapolis Lakers in the mid-'60s, moved them to

L.A. and then sold them for a profit. Speculation had it that he hoped to duplicate the same lucrative plan in Texas.

The problem for Short was that he'd already stripped the Senators/Rangers talent down to the bare bones. Attendance was awful, mostly because the product on the field wasn't much better than Clyde's high school squad. And Short's team was playing in a converted minor-league stadium; two-thirds of its seats were metal outfield bleachers.

The trifecta of lousy baseball, uncomfortable seating and the savage Texas summer heat meant the Rangers had averaged barely more than 8,000 fans per game in 1972. With the team on its way to 105 losses in '73, fans weren't exactly flooding the turnstiles for an opportunity to have their buns welded to the white-hot outfield bleachers.

Short desperately needed something — not just to salvage his bottom line but, more importantly, to dangle in front of the prospective millionaire Texas oilmen he hoped to attract as potential suckers.

Then, like manna from heaven, along came Clyde.

It was the perfect scenario for Short and the Rangers. By virtue of its disastrous 100-loss '72 season, Texas had the first overall selection in the June amateur draft. By happenstance, the consensus No. 1 pick among major-league scouts, general managers and Joe Fan watching the game from the corner barstool was that young left-hander from Houston Westchester High.

Speculation on Clyde's signing bonus ranged all the way up to $150,000, with the figure of $125,000 being widely reported as a record MLB bonus up to that point. Those guessing that high forgot who the owner was.

"I knew they were losing money, so I was afraid to ask for too much," Clyde said later. He settled for a $65,000 bonus, he says, the same amount future Rangers manager Bobby Valentine had signed for five years earlier as the No. 4 overall pick of the Los Angeles Dodgers.

Clyde says his salary was $22,500 annually, $5,000 over the major-league minimum, but he didn't read the contract's fine print. He thought he would be getting all that salary. Nope. It would be pro-rated, so he received just $12,000 for the '73 season. He also got a $7,500 roster bonus.

By comparison to other No. 1 overall picks of that era, that was a lowball figure.

Clyde's father Gene handled the negotiations, and it has been reported for years that the Clydes demanded that David make his debut in the big leagues.

But David Clyde, contacted for this book, says that's just not true.

"Absolutely not," Clyde, 66, insisted. "The only thing we asked was to be placed on the 40-man roster. That meant the Rangers would have to use an option each year that they called me up and that I should be in the big leagues to stay by the time I was 22.

"From what I heard, it was either 'Two starts and send him down,' or 'Just go ahead and shut him down,'" Clyde said. "I had already thrown almost 150 innings at Westchester before the Rangers drafted me."

By the end of the '73 season, Clyde had tacked on another 93.1 innings in the major leagues, giving him a total of 241 innings for the year — at 18 years old. It was criminal overuse, and it would never happen today, at a time when major-league clubs are showing ever-increasing sensitivity to innings pitched and workloads for their young arms.

But, as David Clyde has often pointed out, it was a different world in 1973.

Over the last two decades, when interviewed for stories on the anniversaries of Clyde's historic debut, Whitey Herzog, who turned 91 in 2021, has used words like "travesty" and "tragedy."

Herzog's mandate when he was hired to replace Ted Williams as Rangers manager was to tear down the current roster and rebuild it through the draft, much as he had when he was farm director for the Mets. Clyde was to have been the first huge steppingstone in that restructuring. No one doubted that the project would take years.

"As an 18-year-old kid, he might have been as good or better than anybody I'd ever seen," Herzog told Brad Townsend of the *Morning News* in a profile marking the 40th anniversary of Clyde's debut.

"Short went for the fast buck."

SHORT HAD one more trick up his sleeve in 1973 that would effectively poison Clyde's promising major-league career. With just 16 games left in the season, the beat writers were summoned for a hastily called press conference in the Arlington Stadium press lounge. Short, with Herzog sitting calmly on his left, blithely announced that he was firing Whitey.

A beaming Short was showing no sign of feeling guilty: Whitey had to go so that the owner could hire Billy Martin, who had become available a few days earlier when the Detroit Tigers finally tired of his antics. "I'd fire my grandmother to hire Billy Martin," Short had told Herzog a couple of days earlier.

Herzog, who didn't look all that perturbed himself, said he'd taken the obvious warning to heart and started to pack.

"I'm fired," Herzog told the shocked beat writers at the press conference. "I'm the grandmother."

The news was a punch in the gut for Clyde.

"It was the worst possible thing that could happen to me," Clyde said. "Whitey was big on player development. The man they hired" — Clyde would not say Billy Martin's name in our interview — "did not like young players, did not like pitchers and wanted to be the center of attention."

Billy Martin, said infielder Pete Mackanin, Clyde's roommate in 1973, "liked older, veteran players. He wasn't looking at tomorrow."

Billy Martin's one goal in life was to win, by hook or by crook. He knew how to inspire a team. He was a terrific in-game strategist. But he was also a blazing fireworks extravaganza. The results could be spectacular — but also short-lived and messy.

Clyde started the 1974 season, his first full season in the big leagues, pitching well. Near the end of April and early May, he threw three complete nine-inning games in four starts, including an impressive 6-1 win over the Yankees at Yankee Stadium. His ERA was a sweet 2.45.

It was too much too soon for the now-19-year-old, and his arm and endurance paid the price. He failed to last even five innings in nine of his next 11 starts. Martin had seen enough, and he had no sympathy or patience for the struggling youngster. He had the Rangers in a pennant race; he wanted Clyde gone.

Short, though, refused to send his prodigy down, for reasons that started with dollar signs. The vindictive Martin retaliated by pitching Clyde sporadically, sometimes with long breaks between starts, so he had little chance to develop a rhythm. When it became clear near the end of the season that the Rangers weren't going to catch Oakland, Billy began whispering to reporters that it was Clyde's fault.

One of those reporters was my former colleague, Mike Shropshire. As he walked onto the Rangers' charter flight to Kansas City for the team's final three games of the '74 season, Martin reached out and grabbed his sleeve.

What Martin said, according to Shropshire's book, was: "You know who cost us the pennant? That f---ing little David Clyde, that's who. Put that in your goddamn newspaper."

Martin didn't bother to explain why his teen-age starting pitcher should bear the brunt of the blame for his team's inability to pull off an amazing upset. But Clyde was a handy scapegoat.

"I got caught up in a mess that was not my doing," Clyde told me with the perspective of almost five decades in the rearview mirror. "My manager didn't want me there. I even said in '74 that maybe it would be better for me to go pitch in the minors for a while."

He just didn't say it to the right people.

"Maybe my ego kept me from going to the front office and saying, 'Hey, I want to pitch, and I don't care where it's at,'" Clyde admitted.

~ ~ ~

THERE WAS another aspect to Clyde's struggles, too. As mature as he seemed, he was still just a teen-ager. Although he was happy to leap into it with gusto, he was hardly prepared for the post-game night-life of a major-leaguer. Running with veterans like Clyde Wright, Jim Fregosi and Jim Merritt, not to mention Billy Martin himself, he was way out of his league.

"Where was someone to step in and look after me? I had no one to go to," Clyde said. "Look at the group I was thrown into it with — veteran, older players," Clyde said. "I was even made to feel by my manager that I was kind of one of his guys off the field."

Being one of Billy's guys off the field meant drinking with Billy and his coaches and a few select players after games, fighting a hang-over at the ballpark the next day. It was hardly a lifestyle conducive to staying in peak condition, physically or mentally.

"I won't deny that maybe at times I drank too much, but I was not an alcoholic," Clyde insisted. "I never woke up in the morning searching for a beer or a bottle."

Maybe that because he was too busy looking for a handful of as-pirin and his curveball, which had gone AWOL.

By the end of the 1974 season, Clyde, the "savior" left-hander, was 7-17 after two seasons. In the spring of 1975, the Rangers finally came to their senses and did what should have been done in the first place. Clyde was dispatched to Double-A Pittsfield, Mass. In his first home start there, attendance was 110, a far cry from that magical June day in Texas, when he sold out the ballpark.

Except for a single late-September start for the Rangers, Clyde spent the entire season at Pittsfield, going 12-8 with a 3.07 ERA. He was still struggling with his control, however, walking 94 in 161 innings. And the Rangers — indeed, baseball in general — still hadn't learned how to be cautious with young pitchers' arms: In 22 starts, Clyde rang up 14 complete games.

David Clyde had taken a long, painful road to get where he should have begun in the first place. Worse, the real pain was just getting started.

In the spring of '76, Clyde had surgery to repair a nerve problem in his shoulder, likely a result of pitching so many innings so early in his development. He would never be the same again.

The Rangers exposed him in the Rule 5 draft that year, but no other team showed interest after the injury. He struggled to recover and was eventually traded to Cleveland, along with Willie Horton, for pitcher Tom Buskey and outfielder John Lowenstein in 1978.

By 1980, he was out of major-league baseball for good. He was only 24 years old.

~ ~ ~

HINDSIGHT TELLS us that the short-sightedness of what Short and the Rangers did to Clyde borders on criminal malfeasance, both to David Clyde personally and to the Rangers' franchise overall. Might Clyde, developed properly, have become another Koufax? Another Steve Carlton? A Vida Blue?

If so, we can only imagine how that would have affected the fortunes of a franchise that wouldn't break through to a division championship until two decades later.

Remarkably, Clyde has never seemed bitter about how the Rangers rushed him straight from the playing fields of Westchester High School and aborted what might have been a glorious major-league career.

"I don't like how it went down, but they didn't do anything illegal; they didn't do anything unethical," Clyde told an interviewer in 2003, the 30th anniversary of his debut. "I don't believe they did anything immoral, so why should they be condemned for it? It wasn't the right way to do it, but it's a business, and it happens all the time in the real business world, so that's life."

After all, Clyde had loved the lifestyle, the excitement, the challenge. He was a major-leaguer; it was intoxicating.

"That was long, long ago in a land far, far away," Clyde told the *Morning News'* Brad Townsend almost a decade ago. "How do you describe getting to live your dream? How do you describe something you've dreamed [of] your entire life and all of a sudden you wake up and you're right in the middle of it?"

It was the waking-up part that hurt, and now, almost five decades later, Clyde acknowledges how badly the Rangers bungled things.

"It was a huge mistake, and everybody in baseball realizes it now," Clyde told me. "Hopefully, it will never happen again.

"It's just a huge jump [from high school to the majors]. Only a few players have ever been successful doing that. Al Kaline was able to do it, Bob Feller.

"It's not that the physical part of the game is different, it's the entire mental aspect of it."

~ ~ ~

JUNE 27, 1973, should have been the beginning of an illustrious career for David Eugene Clyde. Instead, it was the beginning of the end. Clyde concluded his major-league career with a 18-33 record and a 4.63 ERA.

Ironically, his last major-league pitch drilled Carl Yastrzemski, the man who once said Clyde had pitched him better than any other young pitcher he had ever faced. The date was Aug. 7, 1979.

That winter Cleveland traded Clyde back to the Rangers, who would give him his outright release on March 31, 1980. He never made it back to Arlington Stadium, the scene of his greatest triumph.

Was David Clyde the savior of the franchise? Perhaps not literally, but certainly, in some intangible ways, yes. He provided that one ingredient that every fanbase must have: hope. Hope is like oxygen for fans: They must believe that no matter how bad the situation might be, eventually it will get better. Until Clyde came to the rescue, the Rangers hadn't been able to deliver that belief.

Short would eventually find a local buyer for the ballclub in 1974 — Fort Worth plastic-pipe millionaire Brad Corbett and partners — and skip town with the money. The trajectory for the Rangers would eventually swing upward. Whitey Herzog would embark on a Hall of Fame managing career with Kansas City and St. Louis.

The only real casualty was the promising career of the teenage boy at the center of it all.

That's not a tragedy; that's a crime.

Chapter 4

THE CONSTANT
Tom Grieve, Mr. Ranger

*T*HE CONFLUENCE of Tom Grieve and the Lone Ranger is one of those life incidents that is steeped in wonder. It has the feel of myth yet is as real and solid as a silver bullet. It is best viewed through the prism of half a century of hindsight.

Who else has spent a lifetime in the Texas Rangers organization? Who else was there on Day One, April 21, 1972, and is still there today?

After all, Tom Grieve was a Ranger before the Texas Rangers existed. A member of the Washington Senators team that became the Texas Rangers, he came back to the franchise after his playing career was over to join the front office, quickly rising to general manager. His next move was to the broadcast chair, where he would earn the sobriquet "Mr. Ranger" and where he continues, albeit on a reduced schedule, today.

Now let's take this a step further, beyond loyalty and longevity: Who else embodies the same indomitable characteristics as the masked rider?

Too much? No, not really. More like destiny.

When it comes to the Texas Rangers franchise, Tom Grieve is the Lone Ranger.

We should have made the connection long ago. It was always there, like a cosmic riddle, right under our noses. Tom Grieve and the Lone Ranger; the Lone Ranger and Tom Grieve ...

TWO MEN WERE hired by Texas Rangers owner Brad Corbett on the last day of the 1979 season. They sat side by side in Corbett's private box at Arlington Stadium that day. Tom Grieve was be-

Tom Grieve, pictured here with Ruben Sierra, moved from the field to the front office to the broadcast booth with the Rangers.

ing hired to sell tickets. Clayton Moore was being asked to be the fictional hero that had made him famous — the Lone Ranger.

After Clayton Moore had left that day, after the last out had been made, after Grieve had shaken hands with Corbett and club president and general manager Eddie Robinson and the three men began to file from the room, out of the corner of his eye Grieve spotted a single small object sitting on the counter near the door.

A silver bullet!

If you grew up watching the Lone Ranger on TV in the 1950s, as I did, and as Tom did, you know that the silver bullet was the Lone Ranger's signature calling card. It was a symbol representing justice, good over evil, uprightness. It was a silent warning to those who would seek to harm others.

"I can still see that bullet sitting there," Grieve says. "I can feel it in my hand. Yet so much time has passed and I've told that story so many times, I sometimes wonder now if it was real or if I just imagined it."

～ ～ ～

THAT SEPTEMBER day when he was summoned to Corbett's box with Robinson was already a special one for Grieve, because it was the moment when he embarked on his dream of working in the Rangers' front office. Sure, it was just a job in group sales to start, but both Robinson and Grieve knew that there was more to Tom's future. Robinson even told Grieve that he could see Tom stepping into his general manager's shoes someday.

Heady stuff for someone who had just played his last professional baseball game at Triple-A Tucson a week earlier. Grieve sat there, thrilled at what he was hearing from Corbett and Robinson.

Then the door opened, and the Lone Ranger walked into the room in full regalia, mask and all.

That's when things became surreal for Grieve.

"Growing up, I'd watched the Lone Ranger every Sunday while eating my dinner," Grieve recalls. "I couldn't imagine what the two of us were doing there together."

He would learn soon enough; he had a ringside seat to the negotiations. Corbett wanted Moore, in the role of the Lone Ranger, to promote the Rangers. They settled on six appearances during the 1980 season at Arlington Stadium at $5,000 each.

Grieve, who had just agreed to a $25,000 annual salary, did the math in his head. Moore was going to be making $5,000 more in six appearances than Tom would working all year long. Then again, thought Grieve, he couldn't ride a magnificent white stallion, or twirl a pair of six-shooters on his fingers.

There was a kicker, though. Corbett had decided Grieve should be the liaison between Moore and the Rangers. His duties would include picking Moore up at the airport when he flew in for his appearances.

Oh, and one more thing...

"He had to have a white horse, and that fell in my lap," Grieve remembers. "I had no idea where to find a white horse. I started calling around and located a family with a small ranch in Benbrook. A lady there said she had a horse that would be perfect" for Moore's first appearance at Arlington Stadium on opening day.

Grieve called Moore, who was staying at the Rodeway Inn next to the stadium, and suggested they take a ride out to Benbrook to see the horse and make sure it was suitable for his purposes before opening day. Moore firmly declined. Instead, he instructed Grieve to have the horse trailered to the Rodeway's parking lot for inspection.

Upon arrival, the horse was unloaded. Moore looked the prospective "Silver" over and gave his approval. It was a cursory inspection at best — Moore hadn't even mounted the horse. That troubled Grieve.

On opening day, Grieve was so nervous he was almost shaking. The plan was for the Lone Ranger and "Silver" to enter through the centerfield gate, then gallop around the warning track to the area behind home plate. Grieve had no idea whether the horse would cooperate, whether the stunt would go off as planned. The thought that kept running through Tom's mind: *Moore had never ridden the horse.*

Just before game time, the announcer directed the crowd's attention to center field. From the loudspeakers around the stadium came the familiar voice of Fred Foy with the intro to the popular radio and TV series:

Hi-yo, Silver! A fiery horse with the speed of light, a cloud of dust and a hearty 'Hi-yo Silver' ... The Lone Ranger!

With his faithful Indian companion, Tonto, the daring and resourceful masked rider of the plains led the fight for law and order in the early Western United States. Nowhere in the pages of history can one find a greater champion of justice.

Return with us now to those thrilling days of yesteryear. From out of the past come the thundering hoofbeats of the great horse Silver. The Lone Ranger rides again!

Grieve held his breath. Then, as the *William Tell Overture* began its familiar clarion call, the centerfield gates flew open and the Lone Ranger and Silver burst into view. The crowd roared. Horse and rider whirled to the right, galloping around the left-field warning track, then down the third-base line. When they reached home plate, the Lone Ranger yanked back on the reins and Silver reared, pawing the air with his hooves. Just like on TV.

"My heart was pounding," Grieve recalls. "It was so exciting."

As far as pre-game entertainment in the Rangers' first half-century, it ranks right up there with Van Cliburn's legendary rendition of *The Star-Spangled Banner* to open The Ballpark in Arlington in 1994.

~ ~ ~

THE FIRST TIME I saw Tom Grieve's overdeveloped sense of fairness reach boiling point came at my expense in 1977. I had written a couple of stories with pointed criticism of the team's free-agent shortstop, Bert Campaneris. Campy had enjoyed a wonderful career with the Kansas City/Oakland A's, leading them to three world championships. He had captured six stolen-base titles and was a six-time All-Star.

By the time he arrived in Texas along with pitcher Doyle Alexander as Corbett's first free-agent signees in 1977, Campy was a "hard" 35 years old. That season, in fact, would be his last as a full-time player. He wasn't horrible; he just wasn't Campy anymore. He stole 27 bases but was caught a whopping 20 times. He made 25 errors.

In just my second year as a full-time Rangers beat writer, trying to establish myself as legit, I took some cutesy cheap shots at the fading star. Grieve took offense.

The interesting thing was how he did it. He didn't yell or scream at me in the clubhouse, as players often did in those days. He just firmly presented his case as to why Campaneris deserved better treatment than he was getting in the local press. Grieve's argument and how he went about it put me on the defensive. When he had to leave for a hitters' meeting, I wasn't ready to concede defeat and waited at his locker to continue the discussion.

I'm still not sure why I stayed. Grieve's temporary departure presented the perfect opportunity to disengage and retreat to the press box with my dignity still somewhat intact. That I didn't bolt spoke to the respect I had for Grieve, who had been the team's Player of the Year in 1976, my first full year on the beat. There was something about his obvious sense of justice and fair play that intrigued me. Our debate about what was and wasn't fair game finally broke off when it was time for the media to clear the clubhouse.

A few days later we were in the dugout at Chicago's old Comiskey Park when the Campaneris conversation resumed. I was growing a bit weary of it, but Grieve sought total capitulation. I held my ground as best I could while looking for a way to escape. Meanwhile, Campaneris himself had wandered over to listen to our exchange and at Grieve's urging chimed in. Turned out I wasn't the only sportswriter Campy felt was being too harsh in print.

"That tall Mexican," Campy said in his strong Cuban accent, "he no like me."

The "tall Mexican," we quickly figured out, was my *Dallas Morning News* buddy Galloway. Grieve and I couldn't help it, we both laughed. Campy's off-the-wall description had finally broken the tension.

Grieve's strong sense of fair play reared again in a much more volatile situation a few weeks later in Detroit. An after-game crowd that included ballplayers and baseball writers had gathered at the Lindell AC (Athletic Club), Detroit's legendary sports hangout not far from Tiger Stadium. The place was so crowded that owner Jimmy Butsicaris had stationed an intimidating bouncer at the back door to bar anyone else from entering.

But a man managed to force his way into the bar past the bouncer, his female companion by his side, and a donnybrook ensued in the middle of the room. The bouncer was whaling away, easily getting the best of it; the woman was screaming for someone to help. Grieve suddenly sprang out of the crowd, grabbed the bouncer's victim from behind and wrestled him out of harm's way. It was an act of mercy and courage, attributes that I would come to realize were simply part of Grieve's makeup.

The frustrated combatant wasn't done, though. He made a beeline outside to the trunk of his car. I was close enough to Butsicaris at that point to see him quickly exchange a pair of brass knuckles for the revolver he had in his pocket. The bouncer grabbed an automatic rifle from behind the bar. They both went outside to confront the unhappy customer. This was getting serious.

Panicked bar patrons scrambled for the relative safety of the restrooms. Others, like me, were too reckless to run but squatted down, cautiously peering out the door to see what would happen next. It was over quickly. With his companion pulling at his arm, the angry customer rightly decided his tire iron was no match for the weaponry he was facing and called it a night.

He was lucky. Grieve had spared him from an even worse beating. Who knows, Tom may have saved his life.

I can still see Grieve leaping into the middle of that fight, not to add to the violence but to try to stop it. Silhouetted for a moment against the neon in the dark room, he looked like an avenger, a comic-book hero.

When I reminded him of the incident these many years later, Grieve seemed to have only a vague memory of it. He brushed off his part in the affair. He had done what needed to be done, that's all. No big deal.

Except … in a room full of men, including at least a dozen other ballplayers, it was Grieve who stepped up. While the rest of us were gawking or looking for cover, he looked to help.

Just like the Lone Ranger.

~ ~ ~

THOMAS ALAN GRIEVE — TAG to his friends — was raised in a well-grounded home, with parents who treated their son and two daughters with love and respect. Fair play was normal behavior, not the exception.

"I can't remember my parents ever doing anything I thought was wrong," he says. "They almost never said anything negative about another person. I know that every situation that came up my parents would say, 'Tell the truth; take responsibility if you did something wrong; do the right thing.'"

Grieve has no tattoos, but those words are etched on his soul, a creed he lives by.

"Tom's parents were very grounded, down-to-earth," Tom's wife Kathy says. "There wasn't a phony bone in their bodies."

Grieve's father Alan was a professional trumpet player who played gigs in New York City during the big-band era. After he returned home to Pittsfield, Mass., he formed the Alan Grieve Orchestra. His band played at Tom's senior prom. Tom's mother Polly played the piano at church.

Tom and Kathy met at the end of their ninth-grade year at a Boys Club summer dance, one of those every-Friday-night things small New England towns often staged for their youth. It was one of those typical parties where the girls dance with each other and the guys stand up against the wall with their hands in their pockets, jingling their change.

Tom and Kathy went to rival junior high schools in Pittsfield but had a friend in common, Bobby. At one of the Friday night dances, Bobby introduced Tom to his friend Kathy.

They didn't dance much, Kathy recalls, maybe a couple of slow dances. Tom's athletic prowess did not carry over to the dance floor.

"We'd lean to the left," she says. "Then we'd lean to the right." (Years later, Tom would practice for weeks so he could dance with his daughter Katie at her wedding.)

Tom and Kathy dated through high school. Tom was the handsome star quarterback, captain of the football, basketball and baseball teams their senior year. Kathy was the cute, perky cheerleader.

Tom was recruited by Michigan to play football and baseball. Kathy enrolled at Mount Holyoke, the oldest women's college in the country. They would marry during Kathy's senior year. Tom had left Michigan after being drafted by the Washington Senators with the sixth overall pick of the 1966 Major League Baseball amateur draft. Baseball would be their life.

Kathy Grieve didn't marry Tom because he was a great athlete. She said "yes" because she could see the man he would grow to be. At 73, and after 52 years of marriage, she still loves her husband's honesty and his loyalty.

"His sense of fairness has become even more prevalent as he has gotten older," she says. "He has added more compassion into that. Everything's not always black or white. There's more gray now."

Like Tom, their sons Tim and Ben both played professional baseball; Ben was drafted second overall by Oakland in the 1994 amateur draft. Yet it is the Grieves' youngest child, Katie, who is most like Tom, Kathy says. Katie is president of the UIL Little League in Fort Worth, the first woman to hold that role. She and her dad were co-managers for her 11-year-old son Sam's team in 2022. The team, of course, is called the Rangers. Good luck to the other managers.

~ ~ ~

ASK TOM GRIEVE about the most memorable highlight of his 48-plus-year association with the Texas Rangers and he will immediately tell you that nothing compares with playing the game.

There were great moments during his time as general manager, of course, such as when the team signed Nolan Ryan at the winter meetings in Atlanta in December 1989. Grieve and manager Bobby Valentine were so excited when Ryan and the team reached an agreement that they walked out of the room and simultaneously leaped into the air for an explosive high-five.

As joyous as that moment was, though, it doesn't come close to the thrill Tom felt when he learned that he was being called up from the team's Triple-A affiliate in Denver to join the Washington Senators in 1970, two years before the team would move to Texas.

"From the time I was old enough to remember, I wanted to be a major-league baseball player," he said. "When I got called up, I asked my manager, Del Wilbur, where the Senators were [playing]. He told me I was going to New York."

There was magic in those words.

Despite growing up in the heart of Red Sox country, Tom had been a Yankees fan since he was 4 years old. A many-times-retold family story concerns a painter the Grieves had hired. When toddler Tom wandered into the room where the workman was mixing his paint, the friendly painter greeted him with, "I'll bet you're a Red Sox fan!"

"No, I'm not!" little Tom retorted fiercely. "I'm a Yankee fan!"

Now here he was, heading to Yankee Stadium — home of Mickey Mantle, Yogi Berra, Whitey Ford, Moose Skowron — to play on the same field as the heroes of his youth.

Grieve couldn't sleep on the red-eye from Denver. He was too excited, too pumped. It didn't matter that he'd been to Yankee Stadium with his father on multiple occasions. This was different.

Arriving about an hour before game time, he suited up and then walked through the tunnel to the dugout and onto the field. Never, he recalls, had a ballpark looked so enormous to him as Yankee Stadium did that day. He marveled at the lineup card with his name printed on it, leading off. He stared at home plate, at the pitcher's mound. It was surreal.

"I would have been better off breaking into the big leagues if I'd been coming from Nebraska and didn't know anything about the players or the history of Yankee Stadium," Grieve recalls. "I was overwhelmed by the feeling of playing where my heroes had played.

"I'd been there before with my father. I'd seen the magnificent view of the stadium, the monuments, Mickey Mantle warming up. But to be hit with that feeling. ... How can I be on this field? I'm just a ballplayer who grew up in Pittsfield, watching these guys play. I can't really be one of them."

As he went to the plate for the first time that day, he walked right past his parents sitting in the front row. The moment was so overpowering he wondered if he would even be able to swing the bat.

His thoughts kept going back to the first game he ever saw in Yankee Stadium. Gene Woodling had homered for the Yanks, though Cleveland had won the game 7-2. What stuck in young Tom Grieve's mind that day was how famed Yankee Stadium announcer Bob Sheppard had announced Mickey Mantle's name with such precision and distinction.

Now bat-ting, for the New York Yan-kees, Numbuh 7, Mickey Man-tle.

"I found myself saying it like that, over and over," Grieve says.

Now here he was, approaching home plate, and Sheppard was announcing *his* name.

"I couldn't hear the fans. My legs were shaking, I was so nervous. And then I hear it ... *Now bat-ting, for the Washington Senuh-tuhs, Numbuh 3, Tom Grieve.* It hit me ... that's exactly how he announced Mickey's name. I'm a big-leaguer."

Now the hard part: He still had to swing the bat.

"My lofty goal was just to not strike out," Grieve says.

He didn't. Facing left-hander Fritz Peterson, Grieve hit a grounder to shortstop. Never had he felt such relief in simply making contact. He would ground out three times that day, and that was OK. There would be other days.

Thirty years later, in 2000, Grieve returned to Yankee Stadium on another momentous day. Roger Clemens was pitching against the Oakland A's, including Tom's son Ben, in the playoffs. Tom made sure to arrive early.

"I went out to the monuments (in left center field) first thing, when it wasn't crowded," he said. "I took my time and remembered those players and what they'd meant to me. It was a moving experience.

"The game started; Ben was batting. To hear Bob Sheppard announce Ben ... it all went full circle from when I was 4 years old, and a painter, mixing his paint, said, 'I'll bet you're a Red Sox fan.'"

Years later, in the Yankee Stadium press lounge, Grieve worked up the courage to tell Bob Sheppard what that had meant to him. The next day Sheppard, then in his 90s, sat down beside Grieve.

"He didn't remember my name, I don't think," Grieve recalled in an excellent profile written by *The Athletic*'s Levi Weaver in December 2020. "But he said, 'Young man, when I got home, I shared that story with my wife, and we both decided that's one of the nicest things that anyone's ever shared with me.'

"It's just a great example that more often than not ... what you're afraid to do is going to mean everything to the other person that you don't think wants to hear a word you're saying."

~ ~ ~

FOUR YEARS into his major-league career and two years after the team had moved to Texas from Washington, Grieve got his very own day of celebration. The Rangers were flying to Boston to play the Red

Sox. The folks from Grieve's hometown of Pittsfield, Mass., were planning to crowd Fenway Park to honor their native son. The Red Sox, playing along, declared May 5, 1974, Tom Grieve Day.

Tom was embarrassed. "Horrified," he would say later. Why was *he* getting his own day at hallowed Fenway Park? He was a platoon player, starting only against left-handed pitchers, and the Red Sox were starting two right-handers, so Grieve didn't even know if he would be playing.

That changed the night before the doubleheader. Grieve was walking past the bar at the Boston Sheraton when he heard Rangers manager Billy Martin calling his name.

"Hey, Grievey, c'mere a minute," Martin said, waving him over. Martin said he knew about the Tom Grieve Day ceremony. The Red Sox were starting Luis Tiant in the first game, Juan Marichal in the nightcap, Martin told Grieve: Who did he want?

"That was Billy," Grieve says. "Billy was the ultimate player's manager. From the time the game started until it ended, there was nobody better. It was what happened after that that was Billy's problem. He had the ability to lift bad teams and make them winners. He just couldn't sustain it long-term."

Grieve got two hits and drove in a couple of runs in the opener as the Rangers won 5-3. The ceremony for Tom Grieve Day was scheduled between games. Grieve's teammates from Pittsfield High's 1966 state championship team, members of the Pittsfield Boys Club and the mayor of Pittsfield assembled on the field. Grieve was escorted to the pitcher's mound as the Fenway announcer called the crowd to attention.

"And now, the mayor of Pittsfield, Evan Dobelle, will present Tom with the keys to the city ... *and the keys to a brand-new Chevrolet!*"

Dobelle pulled a set of car keys from his pocket and handed them to Grieve, who was in a state of shock. Then the mayor leaned over and whispered into Tom's ear: "These are the keys to *my* car. We had to tell the Red Sox we were giving you a car, or they wouldn't let us have Tom Grieve Day. Be sure and give them back to me when we get back to the dugout."

It's a story that gets retold time and again whenever Grieve is back home in Pittsfield, having a beer with his buddies.

Being able to laugh at himself is another of Grieve's sweetest character traits.

~ ~ ~

ONE OF THE THINGS that stood out about Tom Grieve as a general manager was his honesty, something baseball beat writers value almost as much as a 2 ½-hour game. Grieve wasn't going to share state secrets, but as a reporter you could count on the fact that he wasn't going to lie to you either. He shared what he could to help us do our jobs. Though he could get prickly when he sensed that someone was pressing hard for a negative story, he generally remained patient.

He wasn't, however, a saint. I remember having to phone him near midnight one night after a beat writer from a rival paper had posted a breaking news story. I woke Grieve up and asked him if the report was true.

"Revo," he said, adding a few choice epithets, "consider the source." Then he hung up.

When Grieve had taken the job as Rangers group-sales director in 1980, he had no idea where it would lead. He simply wanted to get a foot in the door of the team's front office. The Rangers were a small operation in those days, so it was necessary to be a jack-of-all-trades.

After his six seasons as a player with the Rangers, he and Kathy had both realized they wanted to make Arlington their home. An opportunity to come home to Texas and work in the Rangers' front office was a godsend.

"When I took that job, I never looked past it to what the next job was going to be," Grieve says. "I was terrible at sales. It wasn't a job that I loved, but I knew I had to make the best of it if I was going to have a career in baseball."

After Grieve's year in group-sales purgatory, Corbett's successor Eddie Chiles, who had bought the team from Corbett during a poker game, decided to split up the baseball and business operations. Eddie Robinson would head up the baseball side, and Chiles would bring in Sam Meason to handle business operations (a hire Chiles would come to regret). Robinson told Grieve he could stay where he was or become Joe Klein's assistant in the scouting and minor-league office. Grieve jumped at the chance to make a move.

Three years later, after Robinson and Klein had both been fired, the 36-year-old Grieve became the youngest general manager in baseball history.

Less than a year later, Grieve replaced manager Doug Rader with

Bobby Valentine. Valentine had never managed at any level, but that didn't bother Grieve. Having spent a year with Valentine on the New York Mets' bench, Tom had already decided that if he ever had a chance to hire a manager it would be Bobby V.

But the most important decision he made as Rangers general manager? It wasn't Valentine. Surprisingly, it wasn't even signing Nolan Ryan.

"It's hard to say anything was more impactful than bringing Nolan here," Grieve admits, "but the best decision I made was when I hired Marty Scott as farm director; then I hired Sandy Johnson to be the scouting director.

"Sandy hired Luis Rosa to handle our Latin America scouting — and the success he had with Juan [González], Pudge [Rodríguez], Wilson Álvarez, Sammy Sosa ... He and Marty rebuilt the farm department and from that came the backbone of our team going forward, Steve Comer, Rusty Greer, Mitch Williams [who was used to acquire Rafael Palmeiro], Pete O'Brien, Jerry Browne, Steve Buechele ...

"When you look at how that reshaped our team, Sandy was an integral part of all of that. His impact on the front office was more dramatic than anyone who has ever worked in the Rangers' front office."

~ ~ ~

AFTER BEING REPLACED by Doug Melvin as GM in 1994, Grieve moved to the Rangers' TV booth as a color analyst, where he has become beloved for his honesty and insight. Grieve's style enhances the broadcast in an unobtrusive way that fans have embraced.

Now and then, though, Grieve will show a fiery side, usually in connection with his unshakable sense of fair play. Some will remember that day almost 20 years ago when a foul ball shot back up into the seats at the Ballpark in Arlington. A little boy scrambled for it, but a burly fan leaped over a seat and practically knocked him over to snatch it away.

The man's callous actions drew the Wrath of Grieve in the broadcast booth. Tom went off on the fan in no uncertain terms, calling him "the biggest jerk in the stadium." His outrage, so out-of-character for the normally mild-mannered Grieve, drew an instant positive response from the game's TV viewers. The incident, along with Grieve's righteous indignation, even got airtime on ESPN that night.

This is part and parcel of who Tom Grieve is: Most of the time he's the nicest guy on the planet. But once in a while something happens, and he feels compelled to slip on his white hat and mask and ride to the rescue. He does so with a vengeance.

Grieve's philosophy as a broadcaster is simple: Less is more.

"I look at the game like a fan now," Grieve said. "I tell them what I see, because they're seeing exactly what I am, probably thinking what I am."

He sells himself short, of course. The fact is, he sees the game through a kaleidoscope that the rest of us can only dream about. His view is through a vast prism of experiences as a player, minor-league manager, farm director, general manager and now as a broadcaster/fan. Few broadcasters, if any, can bring all that into play.

SO WHAT happened, you may be wondering, to the silver bullet?

You or I might have pocketed the silver bullet that day in Corbett's suite. We might have had it mounted or framed as a keepsake, a reminder of a day like no other at the ballpark.

Not Tom Grieve. In his mind, it wasn't his to keep.

Tom gently set the bullet back on the counter where he'd found it. Perhaps someone on the cleaning crew picked it up later; no one knows now. The bullet, like the Lone Ranger, simply vanished into the mists of Rangers history.

But that moment, that day, left an indelible mark on Grieve. He has been there from the beginning, for the worst of times and for the best of times, respected, beloved, even revered.

For half a century, a river has run through the Texas Rangers franchise.

Its name is Tom Grieve.

Chapter 5

THE CURSE
Two Seasons in the Twilight Zone

*T*HAT THE GENTLEST *manager in Texas Rangers history would be beaten senseless just days before the start of the 1977 season should have been warning enough of what was coming.*

Still, who could have predicted that the Rangers were about to embark on a 24-month journey into baseball's Twilight Zone? For the next two seasons, the Rangers would meander through a Bermuda Triangle of bizarre ownership decisions, managerial confusion, mental breakdowns and epic brawls.

I would argue that no major-league baseball team, not even the Bronx Zoo Yankees, ever endured such a variety of misadventures as those that befell the Rangers during that two-year window of trial and tribulation. For those of us tasked with documenting the day-to-day triumphs and struggles of the team, it was a whirlwind of epic proportions.

Ironically, the Rangers would also somehow play the best baseball in their history at the time, yet in the end it still wasn't enough to save manager Billy Hunter's job.

And, incredibly, Hunter had been the fourth of five — Five! — different Rangers managers over the course of just two seasons.

I would play a miniscule part in the departure of the most successful manager in Rangers history up to that point. Hindsight and the numbers say I was likely on the wrong side of that equation. Then again, maybe you just had to be there, in that time and in that place, to have a real sense of where the Rangers were and where they seemed to be going.

IT ALL BEGAN WITH BLOOD being spilled on the grass on a gorgeous spring day in central Florida, March 28, 1977 ...

The first punch that morning came out of nowhere, like a lightning strike from the perfectly blue and cloudless skies at Orlando's Tinker Field, spring home of the Minnesota Twins.

There was no warning shout or telltale windup, no menacing karate stance or angry threat. A moment earlier one might have thought the two men were idly discussing the perfect weather, or the value of the drag bunt. The next, Texas Rangers manager Frank Lucchesi, a man as harmless as a spring butterfly, was on the ground, bleeding, semi-conscious.

The first blow, a sharp, explosive right to the face, staggered the 51-year-old Lucchesi. Stunned, Lucchesi sagged, already going down, but not before a wicked left smacked into the right side of his face, crushing his cheekbone. So quick and efficient were Lenny Randle's fists that two more punishing blows landed before the reeling Lucchesi finally sprawled onto the bright green turf, 20 feet in front of the visitors' dugout.

And then Randle, standing over the helpless Lucchesi, rained another volley of punches — four? five? too fast to count — on his defenseless manager. As eyewitness Blackie Sherrod, the famed Dallas sports columnist, would write, "I have seen the hand speed of Sugar Ray Robinson and the cobra strikes of Muhammad Ali, but the flurry of Randle's punches, all landing on the manager's face, must have broken all speed records."

A darkness descended on Randle, Lucchesi and the Rangers that day. Two full seasons would pass before the team could break free from its tentacles. Randle and Lucchesi never would, and there would be collateral damage along the way.

Earlier that morning, as the Rangers' bus made its way from Pompano Beach to Orlando, Randle and outfielder Tom Grieve had sat together near the back. That Lenny Randle was upset was no secret. Not only had promising rookie Bump Wills beaten Randle out for the starting job at second, but Lucchesi had been quoted in Fort Worth and Dallas newspapers as saying he was tired of "$80,000-a-year punks" complaining about their playing time.

His biting comment had come in response to beat writers' questions about Randle's complaints that he wasn't given a fair shot to hold his job. The context, Lucchesi later explained, was that he was in the midst of a manager's most unpleasant spring job: cutting almost a dozen players from the roster, sentencing some of them to $9,000-a-year jobs in the minors.

But Randle, who just happened to make $80,000 a year, had been grousing openly for much of the spring, having gone so far as packing his bags to leave camp a day before the punching incident, until teammates talked him out of it.

A three-year starter at second base, Randle was coming off a poor season in 1976, hitting just .228 and struggling defensively. Meanwhile, Bump Wills, a highly touted prospect and son of Dodgers great Maury Wills, was clearly ready for the big leagues.

Randle had begun referring to himself as "the phantom Ranger."

"They just want to get rid of me," he had told teammates and reporters. "If I wanted to be a reserve, I'd join the National Guard."

The conversation with Grieve that day as the bus headed north on I-95 was light, the usual baseball stuff, until Randle asked a pointed question.

"He said to me, 'What would happen if a player punched a manager?'" Grieve recalled. "I dismissed it as a ridiculous hypothetical question."

What Grieve didn't know was that Randle had asked the same question of other teammates, including pitcher Bert Blyleven. Blyleven had told Randle that it would be a good way to get banned from baseball for life.

"Lenny was a good guy, a popular teammate; everyone liked him. When he said that, it never registered to me that there was one ounce of seriousness in his comment," Grieve said. "But there was. It was a premeditated plan."

Of that there could be no doubt. A day earlier Randle had told Channel 4 sports reporter Allen Stone, "I'm a volcano, getting ready to erupt." Lenny was smiling when he said it, so Stone didn't take it seriously. There'd also been an offhand remark from Randle to one of the beat writers that maybe it was time to start throwing punches.

No one thought Lenny, an intelligent and articulate man who was well-liked by both teammates and reporters, would actually do it.

But Randle had given a glimpse of a violent side three years earlier in Arlington Stadium. Cleveland pitcher Bob Johnson had thrown behind Randle, and manager Billy Martin had signaled for a drag bunt, which would draw the pitcher near the first base line and give Lenny a chance to retaliate. On his way to first base, Randle did just that.

As Johnson ran toward the first-base line to field the ball, Randle veered sharply onto the playing field and deliberately smacked hard into Johnson, knocking him off his feet and triggering an all-out bench-clearing brawl on 10-Cent Beer Night. It would be the precursor to the infamous 10-Cent Beer Night melee in Cleveland's Memorial Stadium five days later.

On this spring day in late March in Florida, Lucchesi hadn't taken the team bus, choosing to drive to Orlando himself. Arriving about the time the Rangers began taking batting practice, he walked onto the field still in his street clothes, dapper in a blue-flowered Hawaiian shirt and gray slacks. He greeted a few scouts in the stands and stopped for a brief private conversation with Baltimore super-scout Jim Russo.

Randle had been hitting in the same batting-practice group as Grieve. After running the bases and rounding third, Randle approached Lucchesi and asked if they could talk. The two moved about midway between the cage and the dugout.

Randle would claim later that Lucchesi had used the word "punk" again — as in "What do you want, punk?" — and the word had triggered his rage. Lucchesi, from his hospital bed, said that was a lie. Indeed, that kind of aggressive posture toward one of his players would have been completely out of character for the mild-mannered Lucchesi.

Randle's earlier remarks had indicated he was already primed and ready to blow. The surprise attack was vicious, a 28-year-old professional athlete in prime condition brutally ambushing a portly, 5-foot-7-inch, 52-year-old man.

Who knows what further damage Randle might have done to his defenseless manager if veteran shortstop Bert Campaneris, four strides away, hadn't shaken off his own shock and rushed to straddle the prone Lucchesi. Campaneris, Sherrod wrote, threw up his arms, trying to fend off Randle.

"Leave me alone!" Randle shouted and took a few steps back. He walked into the dugout and picked up a bat, then dropped it, loped into the outfield and began running wind sprints.

Outfielder Ken Henderson, seeing Lucchesi on the ground bleeding, his right eye already swelling deep purple and red, turned to charge after Randle in fury. Teammates held him back.

Grieve was astonished. He and Lenny were friends. They'd been to each other's condos, shared meals. What Lenny had just done was completely out of character for the man Grieve thought he knew.

Grieve has never shied away from expressing the contempt he felt for what Randle did that day.

"It was the cheapest of shots and a gutless, cowardly thing to do by a finely tuned athlete, who knew karate," Grieve said in an interview for this book.

With Lucchesi on his way to the hospital, general manager Dan O'Brien walked into left field and told Randle to come with him. Randle appeared drained and resigned, but not once did he express remorse for his actions.

"All a man wants is respect," he told reporters later. "I'm no different. I just ran out of cheeks to turn. I guess after all these years he took my passiveness for granted. I was just compulsive. I guess it happens in life."

There was no hint of an apology or regret in his words.

That the target of Randle's fury should have been the well-liked Lucchesi was another jarring aspect of the despicable attack. Lucchesi, in his second year in the position after having replaced Billy Martin in 1975, was considered a player's manager, easygoing, affable. To see him like that, bleeding, eye swollen shut, face bruised and puffy, was difficult for his players.

At the emergency room doctors diagnosed Lucchesi with a fractured right cheekbone that would require plastic surgery. He had a concussion and a lacerated lip. His back and kidneys were bruised. He was flown back to Arlington to undergo surgery and spent a week recovering in the hospital.

Randle was initially suspended indefinitely by commissioner Bowie Kuhn. The players' union filed a grievance on Randle's behalf, and the punishment would later be changed to a 30-day suspension and a $10,000 fine. By then the Rangers had already shipped him to the New York Mets for cash and a player to be named later. He also faced a charge of assault, to which he pleaded no contest and paid a $1,050 fine.

There was an immediate outpouring of support for the Rangers manager from around the country. Lucchesi let it be known that he had turned down an offer from certain Italian friends from Philadelphia, who had called asking if he would like them to "take care of things."

Lucchesi sued Randle, and the case was scheduled for trial in Florida eight months later. Grieve remembers sitting on a bench just outside the courtroom, waiting to be called as a witness.

"I was playing [winter ball] in Venezuela, and I was asked to testify by Frank's lawyers," Grieve recalled. "I was simply going to testify to what I saw. Obviously that conversation [on the bus] was going to be brought up.

"I was going to be the first witness. Lenny and his wife came walking by, and Lenny says, 'Tom f---ing Grieve, my friend.' When he said that, I couldn't wait to get in the courtroom. Five minutes later the doors flew open, and it was over. They'd settled at the last minute."

It was not a happy ending for anyone. Lucchesi didn't want to settle, but it was clear that Randle's lawyers and the players' union were intending to try to paint him as a racist. That strategy would have been vastly unfair — remember, Randle and Wills, the player who was displacing him as second-base starter, were *both* black — but it would have become ugly just the same. Randle agreed to pay Lucchesi's medical bills but not much more.

With the Mets, Randle went on to have the best season of his career as starting third baseman in '77, but he faltered badly in '78. He would drift to the Giants, Pirates, Yankees and Mariners, always followed by the specter of that March morning in Florida. Lucchesi, haunted by the physical beating he took, never fully recovered emotionally. He would lose his job before the All-Star break.

The Rangers' two-year journey into purgatory was off to a hellish start.

~ ~ ~

A MONTH LATER, back in Arlington, fists were flailing again, but this time it wasn't a sneak attack on an unsuspecting victim. This was a full-fledged, all-out brawl between two teams that would spend the season at each other's throats, both literally and in the standings.

The May 8, 1977, melee between the Rangers and the Kansas City Royals was the most dramatic baseball fight I witnessed in four decades of covering major-league baseball. This was no typical push-

and-shove, somebody-hold-me-back-or-I-might-use-harsh-words dance. This was a war.

Lucchesi's physical wounds were still healing, and he'd just been released from the hospital days earlier when he found himself in the middle of a 20-minute maelstrom at Arlington Stadium. This time Frank was attempting to play peacemaker, mostly to no avail. Fortunately, no one popped him on his recently reconstructed right cheekbone in the on-field chaos.

The bad blood between the teams had begun 10 days earlier in Kansas City. Royals right-hander Dennis Leonard had plunked Rangers catcher Jim Sundberg in the third inning. Bert Blyleven, on his way to a complete game 5-0 victory, waited until the ninth to drill KC catcher Darrell Porter.

Considering that Blyleven's control had been impeccable – he'd walked just one – the Porter hit was obviously intentional. Tit for tat. Blyleven went about finishing up his shutout.

A week later at Arlington Stadium, Porter stood over Bump Wills, gloating after the Rangers' rookie second baseman was caught in a rundown between home and third. Juan Beníquez had whiffed on a squeeze bunt attempt, and Wills was trapped. In a futile attempt to get an interference call, Wills had deliberately crashed into Porter before being tagged out roughly by Royals third baseman George Brett.

"It was all I could do; I was trapped," Wills said afterward. "So I tried to bump into him. I wasn't trying to start something. I didn't throw any punch, and I wasn't trying to inflict any harm on him.

"While I was down, Porter made a few remarks. He said, 'How's it feel down there?' I said, 'What?' He said, 'What's it like, laying down there?' I said, 'I made a good baseball play.' He said, 'Yeah, and you're also getting your ass back to the dugout.'"

It was the sight of Porter hovering over the downed Wills and trash-talking that galvanized the Rangers' bench. Willie Horton led the charge, and he wasn't coming to chit-chat.

"That was a cheap thing to do," Horton would say later about Porter. "Here the kid was on the ground and looking like he was hurt, and he pops off to him. Heck, even one of Porter's teammates [Brett] was bent over Bump to see if he was OK. And Porter has to go bad-mouthing him."

When Porter turned around, Horton was standing there glaring, fists clenched.

"I figured I'd better hit him before he hit me," Porter told me a few years later, after he was picked up by the Rangers for his final two big-league seasons.

The battle royal was on. Rangers outfielder Claudell Washington was the on-deck hitter, and he sprinted into the fray, hoping to get a piece of Porter. Individual skirmishes broke out all over the field, some near third base, others at the pitching mound and at home plate, where the Rangers' resident tough guy John Ellis squared off with KC's huge first baseman John Mayberry. Ellis dropped Mayberry to his knees with a spine-rattling straight right; then Brett took a wild swing at Ellis from behind, injuring his own arm in the process.

Horton, meanwhile, was running amok, pursuing Porter in the swarm of players locked in combat and tossing aside anyone who got in his way.

"Willie was so strong he was just one-arming people, throwing them around," said Rangers catcher Sundberg, who confessed that he hugged the diminutive Royals shortstop Freddy Patek, the smallest player in the game at the time, and told him, "Just hold on until this is all over."

Several times during the 20-minute fracas it appeared that the umpires were finally regaining control, only to have confrontations flare up again. One of those came when Rangers coach Pat Corrales circled the pack of players and caught Porter from behind with an elbow to the back of the head.

"Corrales took a lot of cheap shots," Royals manager Whitey Herzog fumed after the game. "I told him he was really a no-good son-of-a-bitch. Here's a coach out there who should be helping calm things down, and he's acting crazy."

When umpire crew chief Larry McCoy informed Lucchesi that Wills, Horton, Washington and Corrales had been ejected on the Rangers' side, while Porter was the only Royal being tossed, the Rangers manager went ballistic, eventually earning his own banishment from McCoy.

Herzog, for his part, was still so furious after the game he suggested that Horton and Washington might have been on drugs.

"I looked into Horton's eyes once, and they were this big," he said, holding his hands up in a plate-sized circle. "He's completely out of his gourd."

Horton, it turned out, had never managed to catch up to Porter during the melee. But even when hostilities had finally begun to cool down, he vowed he wouldn't give up his quest to hunt Porter down.

"I'll catch him, I can promise you that. I'll find out what he's made of," Horton told reporters in the immediate aftermath of the brawl. "I'll catch him in a drugstore, in a parking lot, in a lobby, I don't care. I'll show him what old-school is made of."

Which leads to my postscript to the story:

After the game, Horton called the Kansas City clubhouse, asking for Porter. When the Royals catcher declined to come to the phone, Horton left a message: "Tell him to meet me in the parking lot."

Porter wisely ignored that request. Horton, however, was on a mission, and he wasn't giving up.

Suspecting that there could yet be more action, after I had filed my story for the morning paper, I decided to pay a discreet visit to the Red Apple Lounge at the Rodeway Inn, the Royals' team hotel, next door. Further hostilities seemed unlikely, but with Horton on the prowl, anything could still happen. If nothing else, I'd wind down with a cold one before heading home.

I soon spotted Porter having a drink with a few of his teammates. Surely even Horton wouldn't have the audacity to enter this lion's den, would he?

Five minutes later, in dress slacks and a nicely pressed sports shirt, Willie came striding through the door, cool as you please. He walked in like he owned the place, like a stroll in the park.

Horton glanced around the downstairs bar area but didn't see Porter. He climbed the stairs to a second level commanding the dance floor and stood at the rail, literally looking for trouble.

Meanwhile, at a table directly beneath the glowering Horton, an oblivious Porter sat drinking with teammates. If Horton had simply leaned over the rail and looked straight down, he would have spotted his target. It was a comical scene that could have flipped to calamity at any moment.

Willie finally gave up and departed the Red Apple. The two players never did connect, which was just as well, especially for Porter. When I told Porter that story after he joined the Rangers in 1986, he laughed. "I wanted nothing to do with Willie," he said. "Absolutely nothing."

Sadly, Darrell Porter died of a cocaine overdose in 2002. He was only 50 years old.

~ ~ ~

THE CURSE of '77 was just gearing up. A month later it would claim a familiar victim. Frank Lucchesi had already been physically beaten and emotionally wrecked by Lenny Randle's heinous spring-training attack. It had cost him his confidence and his self-esteem. Now owner Brad Corbett decided to strip Lucchesi of the one thing he had left — his job.

Lucchesi's firing on June 22 would kick off yet another national embarrassment for the Texas Rangers, another dubious "first" for the franchise. The Rangers were about to become the first major-league team ever to have four managers in the span of eight days — three of them in 24 hours.

If the attack on Lucchesi had somehow led to a loss of confidence in him by ownership, neither Brad Corbett nor executive vice president Eddie Robinson would admit it. Robinson wrote in his autobiography "Lucky Me: My Sixty-Five Years in Baseball" that he wasn't sure Lucchesi "ever recovered emotionally from the attack." He was probably right about that.

In any case, the decision to fire Lucchesi seemed premature. The team was exactly .500 at 31-31 and just four games out of first place when he was dismissed. There was still plenty of season left to make up ground, but it would have to be done with someone else at the helm.

Or, as it turned out, three more someone elses.

Corbett would never be mistaken for a patient man. He was always bubbling with energy, over-the-top, fun-loving and emotional; his irrepressible drive had helped him build Robintech, a multimillion-dollar plastic-pipe company in Fort Worth. Now it was fueling his drive for a championship baseball team.

Corbett had eagerly invested in MLB's first free-agent market that off-season, signing right-handed pitcher Doyle Alexander out of Baltimore and shortstop Campaneris, a three-time world champion with Oakland. The Rangers had also traded pitcher Jim Umbarger and infielder Rodney Scott for former Oakland All-Star outfielder Washington and had purchased Horton from Detroit in April to add a power bat to the lineup. Corbett expected to win, but he no longer believed that Lucchesi could deliver on that promise.

Perhaps even worse from Corbett's point of view were the empty seats that were multiplying at Arlington Stadium on a nightly basis. It wasn't even the end of June yet, and already the Rangers were down more than 100,000 in attendance from the '76 season. Corbett and his partners could not afford to take the financial bath that was beginning to seem inevitable.

After beginning the season with a four-game winning streak, the Rangers had muddled their way backward toward .500 as the All-Star Game approached. As the Rangers were dropping 3-of-4 to Seattle in Arlington in mid-June, Corbett had Eddie Robinson draw up a list of potential managerial candidates to replace Lucchesi.

At the top of his short list Robinson wrote the name of Billy Hunter, the longtime Baltimore coach. Just before handing Corbett the list, Robinson scribbled one more name in the margin: Eddie Stanky.

It was more of an afterthought, Robinson admitted later, but the name Stanky still carried gravitas with Corbett and some of the minority owners. Known as "The Brat" during his playing days, Stanky had managed the Cardinals and later the White Sox during the '50s and '60s, neither with much success. He was known for his spunky, hard-nosed attitude and his emphasis on fundamentals.

When Corbett made up his mind about something, he wasted little time moving ahead. As the Rangers were losing 2-1 to the Mariners on the night of June 19, Corbett told Robinson to reach out to Stanky to see if he would be interested in the Rangers job. Stanky lived in Mobile, Ala., where he had been coaching baseball at South Alabama University for the past nine years. He'd had previous offers to return to the major leagues but had turned them all away.

Robinson stepped out of Corbett's Arlington Stadium box and into the team's front-office lobby just across the hall, where receptionist Debbie Cartwright was handling the switchboard. He asked her to try to get Stanky on the phone for him and promptly returned to Corbett's box.

As Cartwright was trying to locate a number for Stanky, *Dallas Times Herald* baseball writer James Walker, walking by in the hall outside, overheard her mention Stanky's name. A few minutes later, Walker knocked on the door to Corbett's box. When Robinson answered, Walker asked him if he was trying to hire Stanky to replace

Frank Lucchesi. Flustered, Robinson told Walker they hadn't even talked to Stanky, which was technically true; that call was still in the works.

Robinson would later write in his book that it was Jim Reeves who showed up at the door to Corbett's box and asked the question about Stanky. Unfortunately, I can't take credit for that. It was good, opportunistic reporting by Walker, who wasn't buying Robinson's denial for a second.

The news that Rangers ownership was looking to make a managerial change and that Stanky was the leading candidate to replace Lucchesi would break in the local papers the next day. Corbett and Robinson, however, said nothing to Lucchesi as the team prepared to kick off a monster 16-game, four-city road trip to Minnesota, California, Oakland and Toronto.

The little skipper who'd been beaten half to death in Orlando less than three months earlier was now dangling in the wind as reports of his imminent firing swirled about him.

When reporters questioned him about the rumors and news reports after the team's arrival in Minneapolis, Lucchesi had no answers. He could only look downcast and confused, appealing to me and the other beat writers to let him know if we heard something definitive before he did.

Corbett and Robinson had gone silent, but the Stanky move was in the works. Here's how Robinson described the situation in his autobiography: "I talked to Stanky the next day [June 20], and he was interested. That day the papers printed the story that we were changing managers and hiring Stanky. The situation was unfair to Frank Lucchesi and not the way we planned it."

Robinson flew to Mobile in director Bill Seay's private plane on June 20 to meet with Stanky, who said he wanted the job but couldn't start for four days due to prior commitments.

"I agreed," Robinson wrote, "but it created a problem because it meant Lucchesi had to suffer through four more days of speculation about his job."

The merciful thing to do at that point would have been to end Lucchesi's misery by announcing an interim manager until Stanky arrived, but that's not how Corbett wanted to do things. Fortunately, it didn't turn out to be four days after all. As the Rangers were losing

Frank Lucchesi, waiting out a rain delay in 1974, was one of four managers in 1977.

the second game of the Minnesota series 9-5 Tuesday night, June 21, Robinson announced that there would be a press conference at the team's Minneapolis hotel the next morning. Obviously, it would be to announce the managerial change.

Minnesota's Metropolitan Stadium was the only venue in the American League at the time that didn't have a visiting manager's office. Lucchesi was forced to dress in the visiting clubhouse, along with the coaches and players. There was no privacy for him as we crowded around him for our interviews after the game.

Frank, in tears, was embarrassed to be weeping in front of his players. Minnesota's visiting clubhouse manager mercifully ushered Lucchesi and the three Texas beat writers into his own tiny office. Frank expressed his disappointment in how the situation had been handled by the Rangers.

"I'm still shocked. If only someone [Corbett or Robinson] in Arlington could have picked up the phone and called me," Lucchesi told us. "Someone should have had the decency to do that. That hurts me deeply."

Lucchesi's paramount concern, he said, was that his family, especially his 14-year-old son Bryan, would be hurt by the way his firing had been mishandled.

"I have a great deal of pride in the game, and my kid [Bryan] has a great deal of pride in his dad."

That night Rangers coach Pat Corrales and I sat up with Lucchesi in his hotel suite until the wee hours of the morning, commiserating and talking about what had happened and what might have been. A bottle of Jack Daniels sat on a side table, mostly untouched. It was a long, unhappy night.

The next day, June 22, Robinson made the official announcement. Lucchesi, still sequestered in his suite at the hotel, declined to attend his own firing. He'd been beaten up enough for one baseball season.

Stanky arrived that afternoon, upbeat and gung-ho about his return to big-league managing. Even though the Rangers played sloppily that night, they still pulled out a 10-8 victory over the Twins. Stanky was off to a 1-0 start as the Rangers' fifth full-time manager.

Robinson, for his part, was simply relieved to have put the Lucchesi mess behind him. On the bus ride back to the hotel that night, Stanky chatted with his coaches about the game and the future. Things finally seemed to be getting back to normal, whatever that might be for the Rangers.

Then, unbelievably, the bottom dropped out.

Robinson was about to head down to breakfast the next morning when the phone rang in his hotel room. It was Stanky on the line, and Robinson invited his new manager to join him in the hotel coffee shop for breakfast.

He was not prepared for Stanky's response.

"Eddie, I apologize, but I can't take the job."

"What do you mean you can't take the job?" Robinson asked as the hairs on the back of his neck began to rise.

"I'm unhappy. I miss my family. I'm at the airport, talking on a pay phone," Stanky replied. "My plane is boarding, and you can't talk me out of it."

Stunned and angry, Robinson said, "Well, if you feel that way, good luck." Then he hung up.

Robinson's was the last of four calls that Stanky had made from the airport that morning. He had also phoned Rangers general manager Dan O'Brien back in Texas, as well as coach Connie Ryan and third baseman Toby Harrah in the team hotel.

"You know, it's really sad for him to leave," Harrah said later. "I was really excited about him coming to the team. I could feel some real enthusiasm building. I liked the way he started right in trying to teach us the first night."

Robinson was still in his room, gathering his wits, when the phone rang again five minutes after he'd hung up with Stanky. It was Yogi Berra, who had been put through to the wrong Eddie after asking for Stanky.

"Yogi, what are you doing calling me at 8 o'clock in the morning?" Robinson asked his old friend and former teammate. Berra, then a coach for the Yankees, explained that he was calling to congratulate Stanky on his new job. Robinson told him that Stanky had just quit.

"You're shittin' me!" Berra exclaimed.

"Yogi, I'm looking for a manager," Robinson said. "You want the job?"

"Hell, no, but I wish you luck," Berra answered.

Robinson and the Rangers would need it. As he pushed around the bacon and eggs on his breakfast plate, Robinson knew that, from an image standpoint, things had just gone from bad to worse for the Texas Rangers. And he still needed a manager.

After finishing breakfast, he phoned Corbett, who was in Kentucky burying his mother, with the bad news. They agreed to make coach Connie Ryan the interim manager until a permanent replacement could be found. Robinson would fly with the team to its next stop in Anaheim. Corbett and O'Brien would meet him in Los Angeles.

Robinson then notified the Texas beat writers of the latest bizarre development. Barely awake, we were shocked, but we didn't have to wonder what our story of the day would be. I immediately went to work on a news story for our evening edition.

As word of Stanky's bailout began to leak out with radio reports back in Texas, phones at all three local newspapers blew up with fans calling to confirm the juicy news and to offer their opinions.

"Homesick? After one day?" said one incredulous caller. "Hell, my wife practically begs me to leave town."

Bobby Bragan, former major-league manager and Fort Worth

icon, was one of the callers to the *Star-Telegram* sports desk. He, too, had tried to phone the Rangers' Minneapolis hotel to offer Stanky congratulations, only to be told by the front desk that Stanky had already checked out. *That's odd,* Bragan had thought; *awfully early for the team to be checking out of the hotel already.*

Whoever answered the phone at the *Star-Telegram* asked if Bragan wanted the job. Nope, Bragan replied, but he had a recommendation: his old Fort Worth Cats buddy Billy Hunter.

Hunter, in his 14th year as the Orioles' third-base coach, had been No. 1 on Robinson's original list. When Robinson caught up with Corbett and O'Brien at Corbett's Beverly Hills Hotel bungalow, he brought Hunter up again. Corbett, it turned out, also wanted to interview retired Twins slugger Harmon Killebrew, who had never managed before.

Corbett, Robinson and O'Brien met with Killebrew at Corbett's bungalow the next day. Killebrew told them he would consider the job only if he could also bring in Cal Ermer, a former Twins manager, as one of his coaches. The Rangers brass was still mulling this over when Killebrew called back the following day and asked to be removed from consideration.

"We just about agreed to everything Saturday night. We told him to sleep on it and we'd sign the contract Sunday," Corbett told reporters after word of the Killebrew courtship spread. "Sunday morning, he balked and said he had second thoughts."

The Rangers brass began experiencing déjà vu. They'd already been down this road with Stanky. They wanted nothing to do with another reluctant manager. Besides, now Connie Ryan was upset that the Rangers might hire Killebrew, with no managerial experience, instead of him.

"If you hire Killebrew, then count me out," Ryan told Corbett. "It means you're just after a name and don't care about the club." If Corbett decided to hire a veteran coach, on the other hand, Ryan indicated he'd stay on.

Corbett was down to two choices: Make Ryan the official manager or offer the job to Billy Hunter. Hunter immediately accepted the Rangers' offer and met the team in Oakland on June 28.

Was Hunter upset that he wasn't the Rangers' first choice — or even second — for the job?

"Why should I be?" Hunter responded. "I'm the one who has the job now."

~ ~ ~

RANDY GALLOWAY, *Dallas Times-Herald* beat writer Paul Hagen and I made the long flight with the team to Toronto on the next Thursday, the only off-day on the trip. After checking into the team hotel, we met in the bar for a drink. Hunter was already there with a couple of his coaches.

It was our first opportunity to be around the new manager away from the ballpark, so I walked around the bar to say hello.

"I'm glad you came over," Hunter said, "instead of that c---sucker."

The bitterness in his voice shocked me. I was doubly baffled when I realized he was talking about beat writer Hagen, who hadn't made it over yet. As far as I knew —and Paul was as much in the dark as I was when I told him what Hunter had said — there was no reason for the new manager's sudden animosity.

But Hunter, we would quickly learn, suffered a distinct change of personality when he was drinking. Calm and reflective, if a bit sarcastic, at the ballpark, he often turned bitter and verbally aggressive when bourbon was involved.

It was a weakness that would play at least a small part in one of the most consequential player-manager showdowns in team history.

The Curse of '77, as it turned out, would have a few more tricks up its sleeve.

Chapter 6

THE MASTER SERGEANT
Back to Basics With Billy Hunter

ONCE THE RANGERS emerged from their disastrous four-man-ager stretch, things settled down under new skipper Billy Hunt-er. Looking ahead to 1978, there was reason to believe it might be the Rangers' best season yet. But then . . .

WHEN BILLY HUNTER took over as Rangers manager in mid-season in 1977, he immediately set about changing the team's culture. He was convinced, and not without reason, that the team needed a different approach from that applied by the easygoing Frank Lucchesi.

Hunter wanted the Rangers to execute the Oriole Way.

Hunter had spent 16 years in Baltimore, much of it as legendary manager Earl Weaver's right-hand man. It was Hunter, not Earl Weaver, who had rightly earned the moniker "Little Hitler" in Baltimore for his no-nonsense approach to teaching fundamentals. It was the foundation for the Orioles' success over the years.

His first order of business was to put the Rangers through an in-season mini spring training with an emphasis on fundamentals. There were drills at 3 in the afternoon before home games. Outfielders and pitchers were running the bases in the hot Texas sun. They didn't especially like it.

"There was a lot of moaning and groaning," catcher Jim Sundberg remembered. "There was a part of Hunter that was very old-school, and it got under the skin of some players."

Like it or not, the extra work was about to pay off. After dropping six of their first 10 games after Hunter's arrival, the Rangers began to roll. Between July 15 and Aug. 12, they won 21 of 26, moving to 16 games over .500 and a game-and-a-half out of first in the AL West. A three-game win streak bumped them into first place, a half-game up on Kansas City, on Aug. 17 and 18.

The Rangers couldn't sustain that torrid pace, though, and the Royals were just heating up. In the middle of August, the Royals blasted off on a 16-game winning streak. They lost a game, then reeled off eight more wins for 24 of 25. By Sept. 25 they were 99-55 and 10 ½ games up in the AL West, and the race was over.

The Rangers would win a Texas franchise record 94 games in '77 and still finish second, eight games behind the scalding-hot Royals. Under Hunter the team was an amazing 60-33. His methods may have been harsh, but the team was winning.

Sundberg was one of the players who flourished under Hunter. A career .223 hitter his first three seasons in the majors, Sundberg hit .291 with a career-high 65 RBIs in '77.

"I think it was confidence, his and mine," Sundberg recalled. "I'd always hit well, over .300, against Baltimore when he was there, so he believed I could hit. Suddenly I wasn't getting pinch-hit for like I had been before.

"He showed confidence in my ability. He left me alone, allowed me to do my thing. For a year there, from about June of '77 to June of '78, I hit over .300."

Sundberg's fondness for Hunter, however, wasn't shared by everyone on the team, and that would become a problem in '78.

～ ～ ～

AFTER THE '77 season ended on a high note, Rangers owner Brad Corbett headed for the Baseball Winter Meetings in Honolulu, ready to do whatever it took to assemble what he believed would be Texas' best team yet. To that end, Corbett almost singlehandedly engineered a four-team, 11-player trade with Atlanta, Pittsburgh and the New York Mets.

Watching it come together was great theater. The four teams' brain trusts had each staked out a corner of a huge ballroom in the Sheraton Waikiki. Corbett was practically sprinting from one corner to the next, throwing out ideas, crafting potential trades, bringing all four teams into his complicated scheme.

Just when it seemed that Corbett was getting hung up on a player's contract and the deal might be stalling, Atlanta's Ted Turner leaped up on a chair and told a red-faced Corbett in his Georgia drawl, "I shoo-uh wouldn't let a little ol' million dollars stand between me and a World Series!" Corbett chomped down on his cigar and went back to work.

The final convoluted package would cost the Rangers pitchers Bert Blyleven, Adrian Devine and Tommy Boggs and outfielders Tom Grieve, Ken Henderson and Eddie Miller. In exchange, the Rangers came away with left-handed pitcher Jon Matlack from the Mets and, from Pittsburgh, perennial .300-hitter Al Oliver along with rookie shortstop Nelson Norman.

As soon as the deal was announced, Corbett made a beeline for the nearest pay phone, a couple of Texas beat writers in his wake. Who was he so intent on calling, we wondered? Maybe Hunter, who hadn't made the trip to Hawaii?

"I'm telling you, it's a great deal," Brad was insisting defensively into the receiver as we caught up. Then he thrust the phone at me.

"Here," he said. "Tell Brad Jr. what a great deal this is."

Brad Jr., back home in Texas, was 14 years old, and his dad, owner of the Texas Rangers, was trying to justify the trade to him. Flustered, I told Brad Jr. it was indeed a wonderful deal and handed the phone back to Corbett.

Then we all trooped up to my hotel room. Now Corbett phoned his manager back in Texas to convey the news that he had just landed a future batting champ, an ace for his pitching rotation and a promising young shortstop. Corbett was so excited he hopped up onto my bed and began jumping up and down. It was a comical picture.

Corbett wasn't finished with his rebuild either. He also signed free-agent outfielder Richie Zisk from the White Sox and a couple of months into the season sent Claudell Washington to Chicago's south side for outfielder Bobby Bonds, a true dual threat who could hit for power and steal bases. (Bobby would often be accompanied by his son, Barry, who loved hanging out with his dad at Arlington Stadium.)

~ ~ ~

WHEN SPRING TRAINING began in 1978, Hunter again heavily emphasized fundamentals, and he may have been even tougher than he'd been the year before. His approach was pure Marine boot camp, and he was the crusty master sergeant.

He also implemented some new rules, including a requirement that the players wear sport coats on road trips and would no longer be allowed to drink in the team hotel's bar, which would be reserved for the manager and coaches.

The latter antiquated rule had been used around baseball for a long time, but it was new for the Rangers. The purpose behind it was to avoid confrontations between manager and players when both had been drinking. Considering Hunter's tendency to turn surly after a few cocktails, it wasn't a bad idea.

Many of the veteran players, however, didn't agree. Pitcher Dock Ellis, being the rebellious sort anyway, began making it his mission in life to defy Hunter.

On one road trip, Ellis showed up in shirtsleeves. When a teammate asked him why he didn't have a jacket, Ellis held up a tiny sport coat made for Barbie's friend Ken.

Ellis, who claimed to have once thrown a no-hitter in Pittsburgh while on LSD, was famous for wearing pink curlers in the clubhouse to keep his Afro in shape. He was also the most profane player I covered in 50 years of sports writing. He could flay the skin off a reporter with his tongue, often for just breathing the same air.

Nonetheless, I grew to like him. Once he realized you weren't going to pee your pants every time he went off on an expletive-filled rant, he could be insightful and highly quotable — if you could work around the obscenities.

Predictably, none of that made Billy Hunter feel any better about Ellis. The collision was inevitable. It was just a matter of when.

~ ~ ~

THE ZISK signing paid almost instant dividends when he lined a walk-off solo home run into the left field seats in the bottom of the ninth in the season opener against the New York Yankees, handing Jon Matlack and the Rangers a 2-1 victory. They would go on to take two of three from the Yanks, and Corbett was grinning from ear to ear.

The smiles vanished soon enough. The Rangers lost their next eight games, for nine of their first 11. They wouldn't see the sunny side of .500 again until almost mid-May. At the All-Star break they were still only a game over .500 — but somehow just 2 ½ games out of the AL West lead.

It was during a May road swing to Seattle and Minnesota when things came to a head between Hunter and Ellis.

After a day game at the Kingdome, the Rangers had a long wait at the airport before taking a commercial flight to Minneapolis. Many of the players, Ellis included, spent several hours in the airport bar, stoking up for the trip. Hunter had also instituted a no-alcohol rule on flights, which kept players from ordering drinks in the air but not necessarily from drinking, as some made a habit of slipping pint bottles of their favorite beverage into briefcases and coat pockets before the flight.

Two buses met the team at the Twin Cities airport, and Hunter and Ellis happened to wind up on the same one. Or perhaps it wasn't a coincidence. Midway through the 30-minute ride to the team hotel, Ellis stood up in the aisle to make an announcement.

"When I get to the hotel, I'm going to the hotel bar," he proclaimed loudly. "Who's with me?" There were a few shouts of agreement from various corners of the darkened bus.

Ellis continued in that vein until Hunter spoke up from his seat at the front of the bus, saying firmly, "Dock, sit down and be quiet."

Raising his decibel level, Ellis turned the confrontation in an entirely new and ugly direction.

"Did everyone hear that? Did everyone hear what the man said to me?" Ellis shouted. "He said, 'Shut up and sit down, boy! Sit down and shut up, n----r!'"

It was an outrageous declaration that silenced everyone. Hunter declined to re-engage. The final minutes of the bus ride were spent in uncomfortable stony silence.

American League teams traveling to Minneapolis in those days stayed at the Leamington Hotel, shabby though it was, because it was owned by former Rangers owner Bob Short. It was so rundown that Boston's Carlton Fisk was said to have killed a bat in his room with his shoe, carried the creature downstairs on a towel and placed it on the front counter with a few choice epithets.

Ellis did indeed show up in the Leamington hotel bar not long after the team checked in. Hunter, wisely, did not. Perhaps he was already in his room, on the phone with Brad Corbett.

It was there in the hotel bar — a fading lounge the players normally avoided — that Ellis uttered his infamous line to the *Times-Herald's*

Paul Hagen, who was scribbling notes on bar napkins.

"He may be Hitler," Ellis told Hagen, "but he ain't gonna make no lampshade out of me."

Then he urged Hagen to write it just like he said it. Being a good reporter, Hagen did just that.

It was a turning point as far as Hunter's iron-fisted hold on the team was concerned. Now that Ellis had successfully challenged him on the bus, the manager lost face with the players.

Hunter had privately asked Corbett to trade Ellis and was told it would happen. It didn't. Either Corbett couldn't find a deal he liked, or he simply didn't want to get rid of a player of whom he was truly fond. Whatever the reason, by failing to back up his manager and get rid of Ellis, Corbett had basically pulled Hunter's teeth. As far as the players were concerned, the manager was now all bark and no bite.

Dock Ellis and other veteran players like Bert Campaneris and John Ellis already had Corbett's ear, and they didn't hide their disdain for Hunter and his methods. Corbett was listening. So were others.

~ ~ ~

CORBETT HAD indeed assembled a talented team, and the Rangers played well in June and even surged into first place in the division for a few days in July, thanks in part to Sundberg's club-record 22-game hitting streak. But just after the All-Star break they went into another tailspin, losing 15 of 20.

By the end of August, the Rangers were clearly out of the division race. A hot streak in September, when they won 18 of 22, helped them climb back into a tie for second place with the Angels, five games back of the Royals at 87-75. That wasn't nearly good enough for Corbett and executive VP Eddie Robinson, who had expected more and were convinced that Hunter had lost the club.

I thought so, too, at the time. Now I'm not so sure. Maybe the club lost him.

What might have happened if Corbett had backed Hunter and traded Ellis, sending a message to the clubhouse that the manager was in charge and there to stay? Ellis, after all, was the leader of the insurrection. Without him there to constantly agitate, might the minor rebellion have fizzled out? There's no way to know, of course, but I keep thinking about Hunter's numbers: 1 ½ seasons, 38 games over .500.

The Rangers were scheduled to close out the season with a three-game road trip to Seattle. Since the team was out of the race, all three local papers decided to sit this one out. None of the beat writers would be making the trip.

At least that was the plan. Things changed when Corbett and Robinson summoned me into the Stadium Club for an off-the-record conversation as the Rangers were closing out their last home stand against the Twins. The executives had heard that none of the writers would be making the trip. That would be a mistake, they emphasized. They urged me to talk my editors into allowing me to join the team in Seattle. They wouldn't say why, but clearly, they expected something big to happen there.

Then, during the same conversation, Corbett asked me if I thought Pat Corrales, who'd been coaching for the Rangers for two years, would make a good manager. Sure, I said. I liked Pat (especially when he was buying the tequila on his birthday every year in the Banyan Room at the Surf Rider in Pompano Beach). Then Robinson quickly interjected his own support for Connie Ryan, the coach who'd been interim manager after Eddie Stanky's defection. It was almost as if he was throwing out a red herring so I wouldn't focus too much on Corrales.

What was absolutely certain was that Hunter's head was on the chopping block, and it was going to roll in the Pacific Northwest. Corbett wanted to make sure his hometown newspaper was there to write about it.

That's why I was the only Rangers beat writer in Seattle when, on the last day of the 1978 season, Billy Hunter was fired and Pat Corrales became the team's fifth manager in two years.

"I still think that Hunter is an outstanding guy. He did an outstanding job for us last year," Corbett said at a noon press conference just a few hours before the first pitch of the last game of the season. "But we knew we had some major dissension problems on the team. We decided we wanted to get off to a fresh start in spring training next year."

He then went on to pointedly talk about how respected Corrales was by the players. The implication that Hunter wasn't was unmistakable.

For his part, Hunter said that Robinson had told him, "It was just the rumbling among the players."

"I'm shocked and disappointed," Hunter told reporters. I was quite pleased at the way things worked out last year, but I've been disenchanted with the way things worked out this season.

"If I had it to do over again, I'd do some things differently," Hunter said. "I wouldn't ignore some problems that I chose to ignore. Players are much more outspoken now. They're independently wealthy, so whether they get fired or not doesn't seem to matter. It doesn't give you much of a lever to do anything about it."

With that, Hunter flew home to Lutherville, Md., and into Rangers history, with 38 games over .500 as a major-league manager. Of the 23 Texas skippers who have managed more than one game, Hunter's .575 winning percentage is still easily the best in club history.

Hunter had every reason to be bitter, to blame Corbett for not backing him up with the players. Instead, he took the high road. He was calm, willing to answer tough questions from the media, even gracious. He walked out the door with a record to be proud of and his head held high.

Corrales would go on to manage two full seasons, plus the one win in Seattle, finishing with a combined record of 160-164, four games below .500 and a winning percentage of .494. He was well-respected by the players, though.

Chapter 7

THE STATUE

The Strange Case of Roger Moret

*O*F ALL THE BIZARRE *episodes that haunted the Rangers in the 1977-'78 seasons, none was as qualified for "The Twilight Zone" as the strange case of pitcher Roger Moret.*

Over a three-week period at the end of spring training in '78, Moret began displaying signs of a mental breakdown, culminating in the only recorded instance of a clinically diagnosed catatonic trance in Major League Baseball history.

Hiding out in the equipment room next to the Rangers clubhouse, I had a bird's-eye view as it all unfolded.

Texas Rangers

Roger Moret

ANY HOPE that the Curse of '77 would find another team to haunt once the calendar turned to another year flew out the window only four days after the 1978 season opener. Notice of its still noxious presence came with the most curious symbolism to date:

A statue.

Only this "statue" had skin that was warm to the touch, blood running in its veins ... and a shower shoe in its hand, held out like a welcoming gift to anyone passing by.

It also had a name: Roger Moret.

It was late afternoon, April 12, 1978, and I'd just plopped down beside Jon Matlack in the Rangers' dugout. Matlack, scheduled to match pitches that night with Detroit phenom Mark "The Bird" Fidrych, seemed subdued as he watched batting practice.

"You been in the clubhouse yet?" he finally asked me.

I shook my head no.

"You should go in and take a look around," he said mysteriously.

Intrigued, I did as he suggested.

My first glance around the clubhouse showed nothing particularly out of the ordinary. In fact, it was practically empty. Only left-handed pitcher Roger Moret occupied the room. I looked more closely. Moret was standing completely still in front of his locker. Thrust out in front of him in one hand was a rubber shower shoe. I studied him from across the room for several minutes, waiting for him to move. He never so much as blinked. I walked over and said hello.

Not a word. He stared back with the emptiest eyes I'd ever seen.

A bit unnerved, I went back out to the dugout and sat down beside Matlack.

"How long has he been like that?" I asked.

"Over an hour now," Matlack said. "That's why I'm out here. It's spooky."

Damn right it was.

It was the beginning of the most bizarre episode in Texas Rangers history. How many other teams have had a player go into a catatonic state in their clubhouse? It was another dubious first for the same team that within the last year had seen a player viciously attack its manager and a record-setting run of four managers in eight days, including one (Eddie Stanky) who stuck around for just one game.

It would also mark one of the strangest nights I would ever spend covering baseball.

Except that I wasn't really covering baseball at all.

I was watching a man have a mental breakdown. No one seemed to know when Moret might finally snap out of it. No one knew what he might do when he did.

His teammates were confused and concerned. They had no idea how to deal with the situation. None of us did.

After batting practice, I watched as some of the players and coaches approached Moret. Pitching coach Sid Hudson got in Moret's face, talking to him loudly in hopes of getting through. Moret never moved.

"He didn't even see me," Hudson said afterwards. "Look at his eyes."

Moments later, Toby Harrah walked over. He sat on a table the players used for autographing baseballs, a few feet in front of his motionless teammate, speaking softly to him.

At last, there seemed to be a connection. Moret ever so slowly squatted down, his first movement in almost an hour. Then, unexpectedly, he took several bunny hops forward until the shower shoe practically hit Harrah in the face. That was it. Toby gave up and moved away.

The beat writers — myself, Randy Galloway and Paul Hagen — commandeered manager Billy Hunter's office as a bunker, peeking out now and then to see if there was any change in the situation. Hunter, who was in and out preparing for the game, was clearly perturbed.

"I don't need any statues," he famously said. "I need pitchers."

Hunter said he was spooked by the possibility of Moret's experiencing a similar episode or worse on the team's charter flight to Boston after the game. What would they be able to do then? What if he became violent?

In fact, Moret did have a history of violent episodes. In retrospect, that the Rangers — and Major League Baseball in general — had seemed to ignore the issue completely is mind-boggling.

Moret had shown signs of future stardom in 1973, working as a swingman for the Red Sox. He posted a brilliant 13-2 record with an MLB leading .867-win percentage and a 3.17 ERA. Still, he couldn't crack Boston's stellar rotation, which was anchored by Luis Tiant and Bill "Spaceman" Lee.

After a disappointing '75 season, the Red Sox decided to trade Moret to Atlanta for left-handed reliever Tom House, whose greatest claim to fame as a player was catching Hank Aaron's 715th home run in the Braves' bullpen.

The success Moret had enjoyed in Boston abandoned him in Atlanta. He struggled on and off the field. The Braves had claimed Moret was having "family problems," but the reality was that his mental issues were escalating rapidly.

There were stories that he pulled a gun on teammate Willie Montañez and accused him of fathering Moret's first child. That incident was followed by a violent seizure in his Atlanta apartment. Montañez stayed with him until help arrived. Finally, there was another violent episode in Pittsburgh that led to Moret's being admitted to New York's Bellevue Hospital. He bragged later that it took six men to get him into a straitjacket.

The Braves would package him along with four others in a trade with the Rangers for star outfielder and 1974 American League MVP Jeff Burroughs. Ironically, the deal was put together by new Texas general manager Eddie Robinson, the same man who had traded for Moret in Atlanta. Robinson would claim he never knew about Moret's troubles with the Braves.

"If I had known anything about problems like that, I would never have traded for him," said Robinson. "I had a good relationship with Roger. I liked him, and I thought he was a good pitcher."

During the incident in the Rangers clubhouse, both Robinson and owner Brad Corbett seemed genuinely concerned about Moret's well-being. But they too were at a loss as to what was happening, so the Rangers sought help from their own medical professionals and from the Arlington Neuropsychiatric Hospital, just a couple of miles west of the stadium.

"There's definitely something wrong with him. Whether it's in his mind or something else, I don't know," Hunter said at the time. "But I don't think my players would appreciate it if they had to stare at a statue all season."

No, there was not a lot of compassion there for a man who was clearly in crisis. Hunter was worried about his team. The players had a game to play. The beat writers, myself included, were worried about their stories. It sounds cold, and it was. But we were all bewildered by this bizarre development, and none of us had any idea how to help.

We were told the press needed to leave the clubhouse. All of us, of course, had been looking forward to seeing Fidrych pitch, so Galloway and Hagen headed to the press box. Not me. Instinct told me the story of the night would be happening right there, and I was determined not to miss it.

Promising Galloway and Hagen I would call in reports to the press box as things progressed, I slipped into the equipment room next to the clubhouse and stayed out of sight. No one noticed.

Using clubhouse manager Joe Macko's desk phone, I called *Star-Telegram* colleague Bob Lindley in the press box. Lindley was on hand to cover the game for our evening edition. I quietly explained what was happening and told him he would need to write the game story for the morning paper, too. I would stay and write the Moret story, however it turned out.

~ ~ ~

THERE HAD BEEN earlier signs that something was amiss with Moret after the Rangers broke training camp in Pompano Beach and began a barnstorming tour back to Arlington. Moret had approached strangers in the Tulsa hotel lobby, grinning foolishly and showing his biceps in a muscle pose. Later, during warmups on the field, he'd had words and a brief physical altercation with teammate Jim Umbarger. Umbarger had no idea what prompted the episode.

When we'd arrived in Austin, where the Rangers were to play the University of Texas at Disch-Falk Field, Moret had approached Billy Hunter as the manager chatted with reporters before the game.

"I don't wanna play here anymore," Moret blurted abruptly.

Hunter thought the pitcher was joking.

"Where do you want to go?" he asked, "Puerto Rico?"

Moret mumbled something and walked away.

A few minutes later Moret waved me over.

"I want to be traded, or I want to be released," he said in his broken English. "I can't play here anymore. I've had a couple of arguments with other pitchers and I'm very unhappy here. I'm no troublemaker, but it's a long season and I don't think I would be happy here.

"I didn't come here to fight; I came to play baseball. I don't want to have enemies, but I have some here. I have friends, too, but it's not good to have enemies. I want the team to win ... but I can't stay. I really want to go. I want to go bad. If he doesn't let me go, I'll go myself."

This came out in bits and pieces as we worked around Moret's language problems and my rudimentary Spanish during a 20-minute interview. Moret was jumpy and on edge the whole time, like someone whose spring was about to pop.

Back in Texas a day later, Rangers' general manager Eddie Robinson met with Moret and announced that the situation had been resolved. But when reporters approached Moret in the clubhouse, he said he might be gone within the next 24 hours.

Twenty-four hours later, he wasn't going anywhere; it was as if he'd been frozen in a block of ice.

From my vantage point in Macko's office — Joe pretended he hadn't seen me sneak in — I tried to keep an eye on what was going on in the clubhouse.

Trainer Bill Zeigler had notified executive vice president Eddie Robinson, who was eating dinner at home, about the Moret situation. Robinson hurried back to the ballpark, where Moret was still standing in front of his locker in his baseball underwear, shower shoe in hand.

In his autobiography, "Lucky Me: My Sixty-Five Years in Baseball," Robinson wrote that it was decided to physically pick Moret up and carry him into the manager's office, where there was a large leather armchair. Moret remained as stiff as a Louisville Slugger. As Robinson continued to talk to him, Moret gradually began to relax, and there were indications that he was listening.

A clubhouse attendant told me that, when Moret began to come out of his trance-like state, he slapped Robinson. That's not something Robinson mentioned in his book.

Meanwhile, owner Brad Corbett; Dr. Bobby Brown, a former major-league player who practiced cardiology in Fort Worth and had served as interim Rangers president in 1974; and team physician Dr. B.J. Mycoskie had arrived, along with Dr. Murray Skaggs, a psychiatrist from the nearby Arlington Neuropsychiatric Center. An injection to partially sedate Moret was administered. It had no effect.

Now that he was finally moving, in fact, Moret was almost frenetic. Dr. Brown followed him around the training room, syringe in hand, hoping a second injection might calm him down. It's difficult to envision that scene: the reserved and dignified Dr. Brown, soon to become American League president, chasing a half-naked man around with loaded syringe in hand.

In the account in his book, Robinson wrote that Moret began hopping backward "like a rabbit." He bounced down the hall from the trainer's room and back into the clubhouse. He jumped up backward onto the valuables trunk, hopped backward onto the table where Harrah had sat earlier and hopped back onto the floor to his locker, where he reached in backward to retrieve his wallet so he could give Robinson his sister's phone number in New York.

Eventually Dr. Brown caught up and was able to inject more sedative. Robinson promised Moret he would give him his release from the club if he would just willingly climb into a waiting ambulance for a trip to the nearby psychiatric hospital. Spotting me lurking at the clubhouse door, Moret leveled a finger in my direction.

"I want to be traded," he said. "You tell them that."

The ambulance was backed up to the double doors that opened out into the players' parking lot. Although only local TV-radio man Doug Vair and I were there, Corbett and Robinson climbed into the ambulance and covered its side windows with their suit coats, as if secrecy now was a priority. Or perhaps they feared a sudden, violent reaction from Moret at the last minute. No matter. By standing at the front of the ambulance, I was able to watch through the windshield as Moret climbed calmly in behind them.

~ ~ ~

MORET WOULD SPEND almost three weeks in the Arlington Neuropsychiatric Center and even did some throwing while he was there. He made a brief return to the Rangers later during the '78 season and appeared in seven games, both as a starter and reliever.

He wasn't pitching well, though, and Robinson soon received another call from Zeigler; Moret was refusing to take his medication.

Robinson phoned the pitcher and warned him that he would be released if he didn't take his pills. Moret refused. True to his word, Robinson gave him his release.

Back in Puerto Rico, Moret pitched well in winter ball and had a tryout with Cleveland in the spring of 1980. The Indians also released him. He never pitched in the big leagues again.

Moret had been a hero in Puerto Rico, so he attempted to resurrect his baseball life there once again. By now, though, his slow spiral into mental illness was starting to accelerate. He often lost focus during games, sometimes making 20 straight pickoff throws to first, or simply walking off the mound in the middle of an inning. Eventually the Santurce Crabbers said enough was enough and gave him his release.

Moret's last baseball address was with the San Juan Senators. It was just a brief stopover before they sent him on his way, too.

"They told me, 'You look all right on the outside, but we don't know what's going on inside you,'" Moret told my *Star-Telegram* colleague Paul Hagen, who flew to Puerto Rico to interview the former Rangers pitcher in February of 1987.

Hagen found Moret in a drug rehab facility in Ponce, P.R., all but penniless, living on $32 a month from the Puerto Rican government. Without baseball, his life had become aimless. His wife had left him. His children were estranged.

"One day I drove my car to the beach and threw my shoes in the water," Moret told Hagen. "'I don't know why. Another day I threw furniture, my stereo and other things out of the window of my house. I don't know. Just crazy things like that. I think my brother or sister called a psychiatric hospital in San Juan. They put me in handcuffs, and I stayed there two months."

He was diagnosed by San Juan psychiatrist Dr. Luis Escabi with chronic undifferentiated schizophrenia, a disease that manifests itself in bouts of paranoia, deep depression, violence and catatonic trances.

Moret sought escape in the haze of five or six joints a day ... until late one afternoon when the cops, guns drawn, surrounded him and friends at a local roadside pig-roasting stand and declared the party over. The police confiscated nine ounces of marijuana; a few months later, Moret pleaded guilty to possession with intent to distribute and was sentenced to five years in prison.

The sentence was later reduced to three years' parole and 10 years' probation. Moret also began receiving his major-league pension in the late '80s. He died of cancer on Dec. 7, 2020, in his hometown of Guayama, P.R. He was 71 years old.

~ ~ ~

IN THE RANGERS' clubhouse that afternoon in early April 1978, the room had been filled with nervous tension in the room. We were all dumbfounded. No one knew what to do or how to handle the situation.

Jokes were whispered about statues. One player walked by, winked, and said, "Just ignore him," as if Moret was playing some badly orchestrated prank on everyone. As if any of us could ignore someone frozen in place, holding a shower shoe. We tittered with laughter, like eighth-graders passing a joint around behind the gym.

Instead of honest concern for Moret's welfare, we thought the situation was funny, even spooky. What would he do next?

Hindered by language and cultural obstacles, none of the beat writers had developed a real relationship with Moret, which wasn't all that unusual with many of the Caribbean players Some teammates — Harrah, a couple of others — seemed concerned, but they were baffled, too. Most just tried to ignore him; first pitch was just around the corner.

This is what mental illness does; it leaves us helpless. We don't know how to cope with it, how to support someone in the throes of a mental breakdown. We don't understand it, so it makes us uncomfortable.

What could we have done? Nothing, really, beyond showing a little compassion. This was a serious illness, a crisis playing out in front of us, and it needed the attention of professionals, which is what the Rangers immediately took steps to provide, once it came to a head. The rest of us were mere bystanders, like the crowd that gathers at the scene of a car wreck, hoping the firefighters can bring the Jaws of Life in time to pry some poor soul out of harm's way.

More than 40 years later, we're accustomed to talking more about mental illness than we did back in the late '70s. We know it's serious business. But it's still a mystery to most of us.

What I still remember is the look on Moret's face that day in Austin, when he came to me to say that he wanted to go home. There was such anguish there, such pain.

I don't know why he thought I could help, why he turned to me that afternoon. I had no answers for him. All I could tell him was to talk to Robinson or Hunter.

It wasn't enough. It never is.

Chapter 8

THE TAHITIAN WARLORD
Riding the Doug Rader Rollercoaster

*P*AT CORRALES FOLLOWED *Billy Hunter as Rangers manager; the players loved him, but he couldn't pull them out of their mediocrity in 1979-1980.*

In 1981, longtime major-league manager/coach Don Zimmer needed one more win to get the Rangers into the expanded playoffs. A players' strike cut the season into two "halves"; had the Rangers won their last game before the work stoppage, they'd have qualified for the post-season. So close and yet so far.

Zimmer's magic disappeared in 1982 when the club collapsed and lost 98 games, their worst showing since 1973, and it cost Zimmer his job. The parting turned nasty when owner Eddie Chiles privately fired the manager on July 26, then asked him to stay on the job for another three days. Zimmer confided in me, and I broke the story 36 hours after the firing.

"You don't fire people and tell 'em to go to work," said Zimmer, who attended the press conference announcing his own fate. "This is something I never heard of in baseball."

Chiles lashed out at the media for meddling in what he considered to be his business, but team captain Buddy Bell summed up the situation best: "It's a shabbily run organization right now. I'm afraid things aren't going forward anymore. They're going backwards. It's like we're an expansion team now."

Chiles and new general manager Joe Klein then went out and hired the man they believed could reverse that trend. It worked, too — for three months, anyway. Welcome to the era of the Tahitian Warlord ...

EVERYTHING IN THE ROOM was red.

Doug Rader's hair.

His florid face.

His deep-scarlet freckles.

The very air around him seemed as though it was glowing red.

Rader's seething fury could have been triggered by the fact that the Rangers had just taken a 5-2 loss to the Royals, or by the fact that it was a fourth straight defeat for his team. None of that was exactly the reason, though.

No, Rader was still enraged because Kansas City's toothpick-chewing second baseman, U L Washington, had declined to provoke an all-out, dugout-clearing seventh-inning brawl that would have given the Rangers manager a chance to maim several players, particularly Washington himself.

You could practically see steam rising from the back of Rader's neck and bulging bare shoulders. The very temperature in the visiting manager's office at Royals Stadium in Kansas City seemed to be climbing.

Into this inferno, like the biblical figures Shadrach, Meshach and Abednego, marched three Rangers beat writers. Sheep to the slaughter. Pigs to the luau.

I took the only chair, across from Rader's desk. Tim Kurkjian of the *Dallas Morning News* and Randy Youngman of the *Dallas Times-Herald* posted up somewhere behind me. Very much aware of Rader's mood, nobody was eager to ask the first question of our postgame interview.

It was May 25, 1983, 42 games into Rader's first season as Rangers manager. We had already learned, sometimes the hard way, that the man who was known as the "Red Rooster" during his time as a tough-as-nails Gold-Glove-winning third baseman for the Houston Astros could be more than a little volatile.

This had all the makings of one of those times.

It had started in the seventh inning, with Kansas City's Washington at bat, when a fastball from Rangers right-hander Danny Darwin had almost clipped the toothpick dangling from Washington's lower lip. The Royals infielder had picked himself up off the dirt and screamed obscenities at the Rangers pitcher. Darwin, who would one day earn the nickname "Dr. Death" for his habit of pitching inside —

meaning *inside a batter's ribcage* — calmly motioned for Washington to continue the debate face-to-face, at the mound.

This was routine baseball theater. Had Washington intended to charge the mound, he would have already done it. Darwin had cordially extended the invitation, and U L had wisely decided not to RSVP. That should have ended it. Back to business.

Except that Rader was going berserk in the visiting dugout. Bellowing — pleading! — for Washington to go to the mound, he was physically attacking a protective metal rail placed to prevent players from tumbling into the dugout. The rail was losing the battle, threatening to come loose from its moorings.

When no on-field combat developed, Rader spent the final two innings pacing the home-plate end of the third-base dugout like a caged lion. He was still hoping that someone would instigate something so that he could rampage onto the field, turning the diamond into his own personal theater of war.

How do you conduct a post-game interview with a man like that?

Very, very carefully.

It was common in those days for a manager to be in various stages of divesting himself of his uniform when reporters came clamoring into his office after games. In this case, Rader had already stripped down to his baseball underwear. He sat behind his desk, seething, waiting for one of us to speak.

As senior beat writer I figured it was my responsibility to break the silence, so I flippantly threw out what I thought would be an innocuous first question.

"U L sure didn't want to go to the mound, did he?" I ventured with a chuckle, hoping to lighten the atmosphere. Instead, it was as if I'd struck a match in a room full of gas fumes.

Rader all but burst into flame. He snatched up one of his size-14 baseball cleats and hurled it into the door behind Kurkjian and Youngman with a velocity Nolan Ryan would have envied. With a roar he swept a massive arm through his dress clothes hanging innocently on a wardrobe rack beside the desk. The clothes scattered into the air like frightened birds.

That's when I went blind.

I literally could not see. Was I dead? Struck blind by fear?

No, something soft had settled over my head, all the way down to my shoulders. It suddenly dawned on me that I was wearing Rader's dress pants, upside down. I could have unzipped them and peeked out, but under the circumstances ...

For a moment, I froze. I wasn't sure I wanted to come out of hiding for fear of triggering another explosion, but I couldn't very well wear a pair of pants on my head forever. I gently lifted Rader's trousers off, folded them carefully and laid them on the desk.

"Give me one shot at him," Rader was fuming, "and I'll break his back."

We hurriedly asked a few routine questions about the game; Rader answered through gritted teeth; and we scurried out meekly, like mice running for cover.

This was life covering the man who once, in the darkness of a late-night flight aboard a Houston Astros charter, mused aloud that he should have been born a Tahitian warlord or a pirate.

He was right. Douglas Lee Rader would have been better suited to a life where the possibility of violence was an everyday circumstance and there were no rules or laws to worry about. Not that he worried about them all that much anyway.

Rader's antics had figured prominently in pitcher Jim Bouton's sequel to his revelatory 1970 sports diary "Ball Four." In "I'm Glad You Didn't Take It Personally," Bouton had devoted almost eight pages to Rader and his behind-the-scenes antics: inviting a teammate and his wife over for dinner and then answering the door in the nude; taking a poop on a teammate's birthday cake in the clubhouse. You know, Tahitian warlord stuff.

THOSE OF US who covered the Rangers for the three major sports sections in Dallas-Fort Worth understood that we'd be getting a unique personality when new Rangers general manager Joe Klein picked Rader out of three finalists to be the Texas manager in 1982. Jim Leyland and Bobby Valentine, the other two finalists, would have to wait a bit longer for their chance.

There was logic behind Klein's decision. Rader, by all accounts, was a brilliant manager.

"Doug Rader is the closest thing to a genius I've ever met in baseball," one of his former coaches, Rich Donnelly, once told national baseball scribe Peter Gammons. "He's like the man of a thousand faces. Or like the Grand Canyon. He can be one thing in one light and be completely different in another. He's tough, but he's soft. He's incredibly thoughtful; then he's incredibly intense. Doug is intense about breakfast."

Rader had been highly successful in managing San Diego's less-than-talented Triple A team in Hawaii, bonding with his players by inviting the whole team over for cookouts or taking them on snorkeling excursions. He didn't even drown anyone.

"As a manager, he could be whatever the situation required him to be," former Angels general manager Mike Port told *Sports Illustrated*'s Ron Fimrite in 2021. Port had worked with Rader in San Diego and later, several years after Rader's stint with the Rangers, hired him to manage the Angels.

"I consider him to be a brilliant individual in so many respects, not just baseball-wise," Port said. "If we required him to be hard-nosed, he could be. If we needed him to be compassionate, he was capable of doing that as well. He was able to put players in a position to succeed."

After the Rangers had sunk into the doldrums under the loveable Don Zimmer and his interim replacement Darrell Johnson in 1982, Klein wanted a motivator for the team. He was looking for "different," for charisma. Rader, he believed, had all that and more.

It was the "more" that was worrisome to some.

On the one hand, Rader claimed when he took the job that the "statute of limitations" had run out on the stories from Bouton's books. But during the same introductory press conference, on Nov. 2, 1982, at Arlington Stadium, he also hinted that he would have no problem using physical force with his players if necessary.

"I'm fairly strong," the 6-3, 240-pound Rader told the assembled media when asked about his motivational tactics, somehow managing a straight face. There were guffaws from the audience. "I'm serious," he said. "I think it's very important for all players to understand that I'm willing to do whatever I have to do as far as what's best for the team. I mean, I will go to *any* lengths."

We can't say we weren't warned. Still, we had no idea what lay ahead.

Much of the time it was just Rader being Rader: eccentric, off-the-wall and essentially harmless. Adopted from a Chicago orphanage at a young age, he referred to his mother as "Meat," though it was obvious that he loved her dearly, often choking up when he spoke about her. Ballplayers the rest of the world knew as Willie — Willie Mays, Willie McCovey, Willie Stargell — were all "Bill" to Rader.

At his first winter meetings as Texas manager, in Honolulu in December of 1982, Rader donned snorkel mask and swim fins one night at the Waikiki Sheraton and proceeded to swim several hundred yards out to sea. Some said it might even have been a mile. Afterward, still in full snorkeling regalia, fins slapping on the tile floor, he strode through the lobby of the hotel dripping wet, flopped down in a chair in the lobby bar and ordered a drink.

This was the funny Rader, the wild and crazy guy, the one who'd made extra money in college by boxing professionally as Lou D'Bardini for 50 bucks a match and playing semi-pro hockey as Dominic Bulganzio.

Why the aliases? "My mom would have killed me if she'd found out, but I needed the money," he explained. The only unbelievable part of the story was Rader's claim that he lost all 20 of his bouts. Not buying that.

There was the charmingly off-the-wall Rader, the manager who, during spring training, arranged for a lunchtime picnic in center field for the players, with hot dogs and all the fixings. That was the same Rader who picked up a homeless man wandering the streets of Pompano Beach, brought him to the ballpark, dressed him in a uniform and introduced him to the bewildered players as the team's new hitting coach.

"We should listen to this guy," center fielder Mickey Rivers insisted after a heart-to-heart with the team's new "coach." "He knows what he's talking about."

But there was a dark side to the new manager, too. When my reporting colleague Steve Pate wrote something Rader didn't like early in the '83 season, Rader told me he was "gonna kill him." He sounded serious enough that I felt compelled to remind him that it wouldn't look good on his next resume.

Losing drove Rader even crazier than he already was. After one egregious loss, Rader burst into the Texas clubhouse, ripped off his jersey and challenged his shocked players to fight, one at a time or all at once. He took their failure as a personal affront.

"He took everything too personally," third baseman Buddy Bell would say later. "He did that a couple of times, as I recall. Later, he'd be smiling, laughing it off. But there would be some collateral damage, and sometimes you can't recoup that."

During one tense game in Chicago's Comiskey Park, Rader called a timeout and walked menacingly toward home plate, motioning to White Sox skipper Tony La Russa to meet him there. La Russa ambled out to the plate, hands stuffed deep in his jacket pockets — who hits a man with his hands in his pockets, right? — and the two men chatted for a minute.

Asked later what he'd said to La Russa, Rader resorted to his default threat: "I told him I'd break his back."

Late in the '83 season, his first with the Rangers, Rader became obsessed with finishing second to the White Sox, who were running away with the division. The Rangers had been in first place at the All-Star break but were fading fast. Rader was still pushing his team hard in September, when the Rangers were in Seattle for a basically meaningless series with the Mariners.

Early on a Sunday morning before an afternoon game, Rader and his coaches were having breakfast in the Seattle Sheraton coffee shop when several players, including veterans Buddy Bell, Larry Parrish and Bucky Dent, walked through the hotel's front door. Anyone could see they were bleary-eyed and just getting in from an all-nighter.

An incensed Rader called a team meeting in the Kingdome outfield before the game and reamed his veterans out in front of the rest of the players. The next day in Oakland, he informed the beat writers about the incident, clearly hoping to embarrass his players in the press.

"A number of guys are just trying to play out the string, and they don't want me to say anything," he said. "They want me to make it easy for them to fail. I won't do that. If somebody makes them play, makes them dedicate themselves, then they get upset. That's just too bad.

"I'm not going to look the other way for them, like other managers may have in the past. I'm not going to let this perpetuate itself. I was hoping we'd have a little more character than we evidently have."

Bell, the team captain, was especially offended by Rader's verbal attack.

"No one has ever said anything like that to me in my career," Bell told the *Morning News'* Tim Kurkjian. "This team doesn't have an attitude problem. It has a talent problem."

It had a manager problem, too, though owner Eddie Chiles and general manager Joe Klein were loath to admit it. Or maybe they were intimidated by Rader, too, because Rader was running roughshod over everyone.

Even prominent *Dallas Morning News* sports editor Dave Smith ran afoul of the "Rooster." Smith had flown to Pompano Beach in the spring of '84 to meet Rader and to talk about how his paper planned to cover the team. Smith took a seat opposite Rader, who was relaxing in his skivvies in his tiny office at Pompano's ancient Municipal Field. Smith's beat writer Tim Kurkjian sat to the side, like a referee at a tennis match.

The discussion between Smith and Rader was amiable enough, until it veered into a somewhat heated back-and-forth over the role of the baseball beat writer. Rader got in the last word(s) with a succinct response to one of the country's most prominent and respected sports editors:

"Eat me."

Smith needn't have worried too much about Tim, though. If Rader had a favorite among the beat writers, it was Kurkjian. *Everybody* loved Tim, and for good reason. He was funny, self-deprecating in his humor, easy to talk to, insightful in his reporting — just some of the reasons for his current popularity as a baseball analyst for ESPN.

Kurkjian's perspective on Rader differs somewhat from that of most other Texas beat writers who covered the team.

"I still think he's one of the most fascinating people I've ever met in baseball — smart, well-read," Kurkjian told me. "There was a crude side to him, too, but I enjoyed him because he had a great sense of humor and didn't take himself too seriously.

"Early on I told him that he reminded me of the cartoon character Foghorn Leghorn. He unbuttoned his baseball pants and showed me that he had 'Foghorn' written on his jock. That was classic Doug Rader."

Kurkjian acknowledges that Rader had a "huge temper" simmering just beneath the surface.

"It made me uncomfortable," he said, "but I just thought it was part of his personality, part of his persona."

Paul Hagen, who covered the Rangers for both the *Times-Herald* and the *Star-Telegram,* sees it another way:

"He was a classic bully who tried to get his way through intimidation," Hagen said.

I can't argue with either of them. Of the 14 full-time Rangers managers I covered as a beat writer and columnist, Rader was far and away the most difficult.

You needn't take my word for it. Phil Rogers, who replaced Youngman on the beat for the *Times-Herald* in June of 1984, wrote in his book "The Impossible Takes a Little Longer" of a post-game confrontation Rader and I had on Rogers' first-ever road trip with the team, in Seattle.

"Rader was wound tight, and after one game he and the *Fort Worth Star-Telegram*'s Jim Reeves got into a shouting match over something that was asked or had been written. Maybe it was the tone of somebody's voice or the color of someone's socks. I'm not exactly sure, and it doesn't really matter. All I know was that the scene was ugly.

"The tension in Rader's office hit you like the first wave of heat from a car that had sat for hours in the August sun. Reeves did not back down to Rader, but there clearly wasn't much pleasure in standing up to him. It was a no-win proposition."

Managers and players occasionally screaming at beat writers is nothing new. As Rogers went on to write, entering a small room with large men and having to ask them why they just screwed up is an unpleasant aspect of the job for both sides. It's understandable that they might not always take it well.

Rader, however, took the art of intimidation to new heights, especially during his last year on the job, when he'd come to the realization that he couldn't make his players do things they simply didn't have the talent to do.

"The day he was fired, it was as if a great weight had been lifted off my shoulders," my colleague Hagen told me. "He was such a control freak, and he really wanted to be able to dictate everything, including what we should write. It was really an uncomfortable experience. I found him very unpleasant to be around."

~ ~ ~

Buddy Bell and Jim Sundberg were easily the team's two most popular players, and Rader had wasted little time in browbeating and alienating both.

Rader never forgave Sundberg for vetoing a trade to the Dodgers at the 1982 winter meetings in Honolulu. The deal would have brought back a haul of talent, including pitchers Orel Hershiser, Burt Hooton and Dave Stewart.

Sundberg, a six-time Gold Glove winner and three-time All-Star, used his veto power to nix the deal because the Dodgers wanted to cut his compensation by about a third. It would have been a great deal for the Rangers — Hershiser was just about to explode as a terrific starting pitcher – but the Dodgers' attempt to rewrite Sundberg's contract was simply unacceptable to him.

Rader didn't care. He just wanted Sundberg gone. Two months after those winter meetings, Rader began his campaign to disparage the fan favorite.

"I've heard that Sunny doesn't always go hard into first base or that he doesn't always round first hard," Rader said in February of '83, before Sundberg had even played a game for him. "I'm going to expect players to go hard at all times."

In April, Rader made an example of Sundberg after a base-running mistake. He regularly ridiculed him for not blocking the plate. It was ridiculously unfair, and it was costing Rader credibility with the players, the fans and even owner Eddie Chiles, who saw the team's attendance slipping badly.

"Rader wanted me to be this guy who would eat nails, to play the game with the same reckless abandon that he played the game," Sundberg told me for this book. "It was all intimidation with him. It was a scary environment, not one which you could thrive in.

"After I nixed the trade, he used every situation to rub my face in the dirt. I was head of the chapel program [Sundberg had arranged for a brief worship service for players on Sundays], and Doug made it where the speaker had to come at a time that made it impossible to do it."

Depressed and under constant pressure, Sundberg hit just .206 in '83, and Rader eventually got his wish when Rangers GM Joe Klein traded the former All-Star to Milwaukee for catcher Ned Yost and minor-league pitcher Dan Scarpetta.

"We made the deal because Yost is a better player. Period. That's it," Rader declared. "I would have traded him even up."

Yost proceeded to hit .182 with a dozen passed balls, developed "excessive eye pressure" that prevented him from wearing contact lenses and was released after one season.

What wasn't publicized at the time was that the Rangers were making overtures to bring Sundberg back. He'd had a decent year with the Brewers, who gave the Rangers permission to talk to him.

"[Rangers president] Mike Stone and Eddie Chiles and I met at a restaurant in downtown Arlington," Sundberg recalled. "They'd taken a beating [in the press] and asked if I would consider coming back. I told them there was something wrong with Rader, and I couldn't do it.

"They asked if I would meet with Rader. I flew in and met with him at one of the airport hotels. It was a cordial meeting, and I looked him in the eye and told him I didn't know if I could trust him. It became obvious it just wasn't going to work."

Milwaukee ultimately traded Sundberg to Kansas City, where he became instrumental in helping the Royals win a World Series in 1985, putting the cherry on top of a fantastic career. In the Royals clubhouse after their championship-clinching victory over the Cardinals, I remember trying to interview Sundberg as he was pouring a bottle of victory champagne over my head. Made it hard to read my notes later in the press box.

The whole unsavory episode with Sundberg and Yost destroyed whatever was left of Rader's credibility and likely hurt Joe Klein's status with Chiles as well.

Klein would be replaced as GM by Tom Grieve with a month left in the '84 season. Grieve inherited a team that would go on to lose 92 games that year and a manager whose intimidating tactics had inflicted damage on the psyches of talented young players like shortstop Jeff Kunkel, reliever Tom Henke and starting pitcher Dave Stewart.

Both Henke and Stewart would go on to have outstanding careers once they were out of Rader's shadow. Stewart didn't escape, however, before an ugly scene in the spring of '85 at Pompano Beach during an exhibition game with Baltimore.

Exhibition games, being essentially meaningless, often serve as a kind of laboratory where pitchers can tinker with their repertoire. Stewart's forkball was getting hammered in this one, which Rader took as a reason to scream at his pitcher. Fuming, Rader went to the mound and ordered Stewart to throw anything but the forkball. When Stewart stubbornly continued to work on the pitch, Rader angrily yanked him from the game. Afterward, the two of them stalked purposefully into Rader's office, slamming the door behind them.

What followed were the distinct sounds of a WWE-style confrontation: bodies slamming into walls, furniture breaking. Stewart finally emerged, still breathing, still in one piece, but essentially done as a Ranger. Neither man would ever talk about what happened inside the office.

The soft-voiced right-hander, however, would eventually wind up in Oakland in 1986, where he strung together four straight seasons of 20-plus wins. The forkball Rader had ordered Stewart not to throw had become unhittable.

~ ~ ~

WINTER MEETINGS in Houston, December 1984: New general manager Tom Grieve is attempting to conduct his first full-scale personnel meeting with the team's front-office executives and scouts, laying out the team's strategy for the upcoming meetings. Manager Doug Rader is lying on a couch in the team's suite, a pile of scouting reports on his lap. He's lifting them up, one by one, saying things like, "No chance on this guy; not a prayer with this guy," and then tossing the reports into the air. They are piling up around him like confetti.

There are 15 to 20 Texas scouts from around different sections of the country in the room, watching Rader warily. *Does he think this is a joke? Will he stop jacking around so they can get some serious work done?*

Grieve, exasperated and embarrassed, finally gives up and ends the meeting, saying they'll try again the next day. As the scouts start filing out, Grieve can't help but hear veteran scout Joe Marchese muttering, "We're fucked; our manager's a jack-off."

Grieve's heart sinks. He has only worked with Rader for a month, at the end of the '84 season, but an uneasy realization sets in: The Rangers are going to need a new manager sooner rather than later.

"It was the first time I'd held that kind of meeting. To act like that at that time, he couldn't show any more disrespect than he did there," Grieve told me in January of 2022. "We were trying to work to create a successful environment for the organization. He was one of our leaders. How could [the scouts] respect him? To me, you couldn't screw up any worse than that."

Not only that, but the Rangers organization was doing its best to ignore the ugly whispers and unofficial reports of Rader's questionable off-field issues.

Like keeping his penis in his pants, for instance.

Almost anyone who was around the Rangers for any length of time in the early '80s knew Rader had an "exposure" problem. I watched him pose for a flash photo in a darkened bar in Ft. Lauderdale one night with his penis hanging out of his trousers. The elderly ladies who were crowding around him for the photo wouldn't realize it until they had the photos printed.

On another occasion, he emerged from the men's room at Smacko's, a tiny but popular post-game hangout in Arlington owned by Rangers clubhouse manager Joe Macko, in the same state.

The late Jennifer Briggs Gerst, a young *Star-Telegram* reporter and former Rangers bat girl, gasped. "Is that real?" she blurted out to her table companions. She'd thought at first it might just be a rubber fake — another of Rader's pranks.

Indeed, it was all too real.

Rader proudly kept a photo of himself and three playing companions at a charity golf tournament taped on the wall in his clubhouse office. His privates were exposed in the photo for all to inspect. It was particularly disconcerting to see owner Eddie Chiles' gray head nodding just under that photo whenever he happened to visit the manager's office. Eddie's eyesight wasn't the greatest by that time, so I doubt he ever noticed what was practically sticking in his ear.

ON MANY occasions over the years since his firing from the Rangers in May of 1985, Rader has expressed regret for how he handled his first major-league managerial opportunity. Interviewed for two excellent profiles, one by Peter Gammons after Rader was named Los Angeles Angels manager in 1989, the other written by *Sports Illustrated*'s Ron Fimrite 30 years later, Rader sounded genuinely sorry and said he had learned much from the experience.

"It got to the point where they expected me to act like an ass, and I did," Rader told Gammons. "When I was finally fired, I was actually relieved. I was totally exhausted, and so was everyone around me."

Buddy Bell, now a vice president and assistant to the general manager with the Cincinnati Reds, where his son David manages, looks back at his two seasons under Rader with mixed emotions. He and Rader have talked about those years on several occasions since, Bell says, adding that Rader has expressed regret for how he handled some situations.

"I thought Doug was one of the most brilliant people I've ever been around," Bell said from Arizona in February 2022. "There were some things that maybe he would have done a little bit differently, especially the way he handled the veteran guys.

"In baseball, if you're not doing good it's the worst damn thing in the world, and you don't need somebody hounding you about it. It was hard on everybody, especially on Doug, because he just couldn't motivate us to be a better team.

"*Everybody* hated losing. Doug seemed to think that he was the only one who really cared. That doesn't go over well."

Rader despised losing — at bridge, at baseball, at anything — as much as anyone I've ever seen. His rage when he couldn't elevate his players through sheer will and determination was too often uncontrollable.

According to Gammons' profile of Rader, after the U L Washington incident and the blowup that ended with me wearing his pants on my head in the Kansas City stadium, Rader told coach Rich Donnelly that he was going to hike the six miles back to the hotel. Then Rader took off his boots and socks and handed them to Donnelly.

"I've got to punish myself," Rader said.

By the time he had trekked the six miles to the hotel, his bare soles were raw and blistered.

They were, I imagine, on fire.

Chapter 9

THE BALLROOM DANCER
The Passion and Persistence of Bobby Valentine

I T WAS BEFORE DAWN, still dark, when loud pounding at his back door woke Bobby Valentine.

"Mucho problema!" Valentine's handyman and stableboy Martín kept repeating. "Mucho problema!" Big problem. He gestured towards the barn and pasture behind the house.

Together the two men walked quickly through the rain to the back deck.

In the dim pre-dawn light, the Texas Rangers manager looked out over his 23-acre spread in east Fort Worth. Instead of a wide grassy pasture, he saw a broad muddy river. Flowing swiftly through the middle of his property, it carried broken limbs and uprooted trees, debris of all kinds.

Yeah, Valentine thought. Big, big problem.

Valentine hurried down to the barn, where every morning Martín would bang the feed bucket and the Valentines' three horses would come trotting up for their breakfast. In the distance, he could just make out two of the horses. They were in chest-deep water, looking for higher ground.

It was May 17, 1989. East Fort Worth and Arlington would be deluged with 13-plus inches of rain that day. It had been pouring for hours. Most of the Valentines' property was in a flood zone. Neighbors had told them not to worry, it was a hundred-year flood plain. Problem was, this *was* the hundred-year flood, and it was a doozy.

There was no way for Valentine to reach the horses from where he was. Then he saw a KVIL news helicopter flying overhead. Valentine ran inside and called the station in Dallas. He asked if the chopper could land in the cul-de-sac in front of his house and then airlift him to the horses. They agreed.

Valentine changed quickly into shorts and running shoes, grabbed rope and halters. A neighbor handed him a walkie-talkie as he boarded the chopper. The helicopter couldn't land next to the frightened horses because of the rushing water but hovered near them, low enough for Valentine to leap out.

He managed to get the halters on the horses — no easy task — and then faced the challenge of leading them back to the barn.

"I thought I would just be able to walk them back to the barn," he remembered in an interview for this book. "But then I realized that the water in front of us was over my head. I decided to try and walk them to the highway, but we got lost in the woods because the trails I was looking for were all under four feet of water."

Former Rangers pitcher Jon Matlack's teen-age daughter came to the rescue. Matlack's property was just southwest of Valentine's, and she had seen the TV clips of Bobby's dramatic attempt to save his horses. She mounted her own horse and rode up and down a ridge with a bullhorn, shouting Valentine's name.

On a day of heroes, count her among them.

"I was able to follow her voice and eventually find my way back," Valentine said.

What he saw when he got back to his barn sent chills up and down his spine. His wife Mary was waist-deep in the flood with two friends. They were trying to get to Bobby Jr.'s Welsh pony, Cinnamon Stitch. The torrent had swept the blind 15-year-old pony into a pipe fence that crossed the pasture. A front leg, caught between rails, had snapped as the flood catapulted her head-first over the fence. The wounded pony drowned in front of the Valentines, who were helpless to reach her. Her body was swept to the far side of the pasture, where it hung up in the trees.

They could not let 4-year-old Bobby Jr. see his beloved Cinny like this. Valentine and his neighbor Pat Marchenke forded the river by carefully crossing on one of the three-rail pipe fences that ran north and south across the pasture, staying on the upstream side to keep from being swept away. Then they started working their way west through the trees to get to the pony.

That's when I entered the picture.

At home in south Arlington, I'd seen the TV coverage of Valentine's heroic effort to save his horses. To paraphrase Robert Duvall's Lt. Col. Kilgore in "Apocalypse Now," I love the smell of a good story in the morning. I drove to Valentine's place in far east Fort Worth as fast as I could.

When I arrived, Bobby and Marchenke were on the far side of the rampaging flood, attempting to maneuver Cinny's body through a web of tree limbs and vines, fighting the current that one moment helped hold her fast and the next threatened to tear her away. They were in chest-deep water, but it was deeper and flowing dangerously faster in the center of the pasture.

I made up my mind quickly. The story was on the other side of the flood with the two men who could obviously use another hand. That was where I needed to be, and maybe I could help Valentine and Marchenke free Cinny, too.

A well-known journalism tradition says that reporters are not supposed to become part of the story. But sometimes, in a crisis, being human must take precedence over everything else. I would worry about the rest later.

Like Valentine and Marchenke before me, I began sidling along the pipe fence, one step at a time, holding onto the top rail tightly as the surge pounded at my back and legs. I remember Valentine shouting, "Revo, go back! I don't want to be responsible!"

I yelled back that I'd been responsible for myself for some years now and kept going. The water was filthy with debris and studded with large islands of fire-ant colonies floating on top. I kept an eye out for broken tree limbs, some of them big enough to knock me off the fence if they hit me.

Once across, I worked my way back west against the current and joined the others. The three of us managed to unwedge the pony and began guiding her body back toward the pasture. She floated easily. We couldn't take her directly across the powerful flow to the other side; she would have been swept away. We would have to use the fence again.

As we emerged from the tree line, the rushing water grabbed her. We couldn't fight the current as it tore her body away from us. I latched on, "riding" her down to the fence, maybe a hundred yards away, hoping I could keep her from being swept over. She bumped up against the fence, and the force of the water held us there.

From that point, we could edge her body down the fence line toward the calmer water closer to the barn. Valentine and Marchenke used a couple of backhoes to dig a grave and bury her. Bobby Jr. would never have to see her body.

When I wrote the story for the next day's paper, I decided not to mention that I was involved in the rescue. My tale, spread across the top of the front page, was told completely from Valentine's perspective, a father desperate to salvage something from a terrible day.

Worse things happened that day than a little boy losing his favorite pony. Three people in the Metroplex died from the flooding. Property was destroyed and millions of dollars in damage done.

But the saga of Valentine and his horses playing out on local television, along with my detailed look at what the Rangers manager had been through, gave viewers and readers a different perspective of a popular local sports figure and captured the hearts of thousands.

"That day will always live in my mind," Valentine told me from his home in Connecticut. "I just remember getting finished in time to shower and go to the ballpark. I don't remember anything that happened in the game that night."

A week or two later I was in the doctor's office, getting debris, dead ants and who knows what flushed out of my clogged-up ears. It was completely worth it, though. You don't get to tell a story like that every day.

~ ~ ~

ON THE DAY he was officially hired as manager of the Texas Rangers in 1985, Bobby Valentine made an unusual entrance into the visitors' clubhouse at Chicago's Comiskey Park. He stepped through the doors, then did two or three perfect dance pirouettes to the center of the room.

My first thought: *My kind of guy.* My second: *How many major-league managers have introduced themselves like that?* I didn't know at the time that Valentine had been a championship competitive ballroom dancer in his youth, not something you'd be likely to find on most sports managers' resumés.

Like so many others who had been at the helm of the Texas Rangers in their brief history, Bobby Valentine was no ordinary major-league manager.

Though he had never managed before, not even in the minors, Valentine was already part baseball genius, part Hollywood star. He brought Tommy Lasorda's gift of gab tempered with a Frankie Avalon smile and Dale Carnegie charm.

Most importantly, he brought hope to a beleaguered fan base and media beaten down by the depressing Doug Rader era. Valentine wasn't just a breath of fresh air; he was a whirlwind of youthful energy and innovation. He wasn't just willing to try new things — pitchers throwing footballs, video scouting, sabermetrics — he enthusiastically embraced them.

It would not be difficult to make the case that it was Valentine, in his seven-plus years as manager, who was the catalyst that changed the Rangers from American League laughingstock to viable major-league franchise.

Valentine was quotable, opinionated and, like Lasorda, loudly Italian. His frank, direct honesty could occasionally cross the line into smart-ass snarkiness, and the fact that he deployed it when he should have been more discreet often made him a polarizing figure. As he admits in his 2021 autobiography "Valentine's Way: My Adventurous Life and Times," his mouth was often his worst enemy. Based on some of his pointed and unfiltered observations in the book, it may still be.

Even as a manager he was a classic bench jockey, loudly needling opposing pitchers mercilessly in hopes of throwing them off their game. This made him no friends in the other dugout, where his antics were detested by many opposing managers and players. Valentine didn't seem to notice. He had a ballgame to win, and that was all that mattered.

"If you didn't know him and you were in the other dugout, I can see where you might not have liked him," said Tom Grieve, the general manager who hired Valentine in May of 1985. "I don't think he has ever been embarrassed a day in his life. He was going to be on the top step of the dugout, his chest stuck out, and he was going to be barking. He was confident in his knowledge of the game, and he was being a leader. I liked that."

Grieve, in fact, had liked Valentine from the moment they met after owner Brad Corbett traded Grieve to the New York Mets in December 1977. Valentine, a reserve outfielder, was the first to welcome

Grieve to his new team, and the two bonded quickly, especially since they both spent most games on the bench. That gave them the chance to think along with the managers, both theirs and the other teams'. They talked strategy almost endlessly.

"It was the kind of thing where we would constantly talk baseball, from the first inning on. What would the manager do here? What would he do in that situation?" Grieve said. "I realized quickly that this guy knows the game on a higher level than I do.

"One day we were on the back field, doing some base-running drills. It was kind of a general tutorial on how to run the bases, and our instructor was Willie Mays, who was a spring training coach."

The Hall of Famer, Grieve recalled, was showing the players how to round first base, pushing off with their right foot on the inside of the bag.

"The next day he said he'd been thinking about it and preferred to touch first with his left foot and cross over with the right. Then he turned to Bobby and asked him how they did it with the Dodgers."

At that point, Grieve said, Valentine proceeded to take over the whole base-running drill, showing the Mets players how the Dodgers did things at each base.

"Willie just stepped back and let him go," Grieve said. "Bobby was that good."

~ ~ ~

BOBBY VALENTINE was easily the hardest-working manager I ever covered. In his first spring training with the Rangers, he had to cope with the dilapidated Municipal Field in Pompano Beach. It was literally falling apart.

The first day he saw the park, Valentine realized there was no netting on the Rangers' batting cage down the right field line. It was too late to order proper netting, so Valentine jumped in his rental car and began driving down A1A, the coastal highway, stopping at marinas and piers when he saw commercial fishing boats. Eventually he found a fisherman willing to sell him all the fish netting he could carry for $50.

Hurrying back to Pompano, Valentine, whose father Joe had been a carpenter, worked until almost dark putting up the netting for the batting cage. When Valentine and the Rangers showed up the next day for their first spring practice, the netting was gone, stolen overnight.

On another occasion, Valentine worked tirelessly to get the field in shape after an overnight rain when the two city workers who looked after the field had forgotten to put the tarp out. When the first batter stepped up, the home plate umpire said, "We can't play this game. The basepath where the runner leads off at first is too wet."

Valentine sprang out of the home dugout and shouted, "Time out!" Then he ran to a nearby mound of red clay and scooped it up in his arms, intending to dump it on the basepath puddle. Halfway there, Valentine yelped and tossed the red clay into the air. Turned out he'd grabbed up a fire ant mound.

Back in Texas, Valentine threw himself into selling the Texas Rangers to the Metroplex. He spoke at Rotary Club breakfasts and Kiwanis luncheons, traveled on every Rangers caravan. He was practically talking Rangers on every street corner in the entire DFW area.

"Tom told me when I was hired that we had a lot of work to do in the community," Valentine said. "God bless [Rangers baseball ambassador] Bobby Bragan that he was there to accompany to so many events and places to introduce me and teach me not only about baseball but what was happening in the Metroplex."

The Rangers offered other resources for Valentine, too, like longtime baseball wizard Paul Richards, special assistant to the general manager, and sabermetrics analyst Craig Wright, both legacies of Eddie Robinson. Valentine had the courage to hire innovative pitching coach Tom House, who was on the cutting edge of biomechanics.

"Some didn't see the compassion Bobby had, the genuine love of the game that he had, the things he would do to help friends," Grieve said. "I also appreciated that no one in the history of baseball so tirelessly worked his ass off. He would drive anywhere to talk about the Rangers or baseball. Whatever we paid him, he should have earned three times that much, just from the time he put in."

~ ~ ~

WHILE "V-BALL," a popular nickname for the Rangers' style of play under Valentine, was taking hold in Arlington, the entire sports world was in the midst of major changes. A new TV network, dedicated entirely to sports, was finding its legs. It was called ESPN. Talk radio was climbing out of its diapers and growing teeth … and Valentine's pitchers were warming up with footballs.

Why? Because pitching coach House had discovered that throwing a football exactly mimicked the proper throwing motion that a pitcher needed to make. Other managers, media and fans thought the Rangers were crazy for doing such untraditional things.

"Throwing the football in the outfield, pitchers lifting weights to build strength, was so frowned on at the time," Valentine said. "I remember having the players practice in shorts, and we had players like Larry Parrish who wouldn't do it because it wasn't traditional. It was simply a way to preserve energy for the game that night."

Meanwhile, hitting coach Tom Robson was talking to his hitters about "launch angle," a way of thinking about hitting that he had adopted from none other than Ted Williams. Today, it's a major element of baseball analytics.

Valentine loved it all, loved Arlington so much that just a couple of years into his managing tenure in Texas he opened two Bobby Valentine Sports Gallery Cafes, one on the north side of Arlington not far from the stadium and another on the south side (still operating with the same name and concept, though Valentine no longer owns it). They were the city's first real sports bars, modeled after Valentine's bar/restaurants in Connecticut, filled with sports memorabilia worth tens of thousands of dollars.

You could often find Valentine in one or the other of his two sports bars almost every day, having lunch with Steve Buechele or Geno Petralli, pulling draft beers, serving nachos and visiting with fans after games until midnight or later.

"I thought it was a spectacular seven-year juncture in my life," he said. "I got there unaware of anything about Texas. When I left, I felt I knew everything Texas.

"We went from seeing Inky (Pete Incaviglia) line a ball through that crumbling plywood fence in Pompano Beach to a brand-new facility in Port Charlotte. We became a real franchise, competing with the Oakland A's and their Hall of Famers, and we were doing it with a lot of homegrown talent.

"We were legitimate enough to lure Nolan Ryan [from the Houston Astros], who pitched some of his greatest seasons for the Rangers. The whole thing was magical. It was the beginning of video scouting, the weight-lifting era, the steroids era. We weren't quite championship caliber over 162 games, but there were three or four times a week when we were as good as any team in baseball most of those years."

It's entirely possible, in fact, that it was Valentine who said the magic words that would put Nolan Ryan in a Rangers uniform for five of the most exciting years Rangers fans ever witnessed. He said them at the Baseball Winter Meetings in Atlanta in December of 1988, and not to Nolan, but to the Ryan household's straw boss: wife Ruth.

Until that meeting, it had looked like Ryan would be returning to the Angels and his friend owner Gene Autry, who had made a very nice offer.

Valentine had played with Ryan in Anaheim. In fact, he was in center field for the Angels when Ryan threw his first no-hitter in 1973. He knew Ruth, too, so while Rangers' team president Mike Stone and Tom Grieve were meeting in the Ryan suite at the winter meetings headquarters hotel with Ryan's agent Dick Moss and Nolan, Bobby walked into the next room to chat with Ruth.

The conversation was casual until Ruth asked a pointed question: How did the Rangers feel about the Ryan boys — Reid and Reese — being in the clubhouse? At the time, the Astros had a rule that players' families weren't allowed in the clubhouse.

"Clubhouse?" Valentine said incredulously. "Heck, they can use my office! They can fly on the team plane if they want to!"

It's difficult to know precisely how much impact that had on the negotiations. But the Ryans wanted to stay in Texas. Their decision to do just that shocked the baseball world. And, at the press conference announcing his signing, Ryan made a point of mentioning how important the Rangers' openness to his family was to him.

AFTER VALENTINE'S hiring in 1985, the Rangers had finished the 1985 season at 53-76. Overall, they were 62-99. A year later, V-Ball was the hottest ticket in town. Fans loved the team's youth movement, led by Rubén Sierra, Pete Incaviglia, Steve Buechele and Oddibe Mc-Dowell, with Edwin Correa and José Guzmán bright young stars in the rotation.

Valentine was so invested, so passionate about his young Rangers that he led the majors in ejections, having been thrown out six times in 1986. The Rangers would finish 87-75, five games back of the AL West champion California Angels. Like his team, Valentine finished second in the race for American League manager of the year.

Rookie outfielder Pete Incaviglia slugged 30 home runs. Larry

Parrish added 28 homers and 94 runs batted in. First baseman Pete O'Brien hit .290 with 23 homers and 90 RBIs. Knuckleballer Charlie Hough led the pitching staff with 17 wins. Young hurlers Edwin Correa, Bobby Witt and Jose Guzman provided hope for the future.

What Tom Grieve remembers is the final game of that season at Arlington Stadium and the emotional outpouring from both the players and the fans. The Rangers had defeated the Angels 7-4 that early October afternoon, having won 12 of their final 16 games. At the time, it seemed like a promise of even better times ahead.

As the shadows lengthened across the field, many of the 20,000 fans in attendance that day refused to leave, standing and cheering, some even weeping. The Rangers players responded in kind. They circled the field, paying homage to the fans and spontaneously tossing their jerseys into the stands. Valentine took the microphone and shouted, "You ain't seen nothing yet!"

It was poignant and heartfelt on both sides, a mutual-admiration society.

"It's something I'll never forget," Grieve said.

The Rangers would finish over .500 in four of Valentine's six full seasons as manager. They were four games over .500 at 45-41 when he was fired in 1992. But it never got better than it did that final day of the '86 season.

IT HAS to be said that the Rangers' successes during that heady period were sprinkled with strikeouts, too.

In 1987, on the recommendation of the Dodgers' Lasorda and Joe Ferguson, Valentine convinced Chiles and Grieve to take a chance on drug-troubled reliever Steve Howe. MLB Commissioner Peter Ueberroth agreed to the deal only with the provision that the Rangers would promise to pay a hefty fine — $250,000 — if Howe went south again. Howe had a brilliant half season with the Rangers, then fell off the wagon — hard.

During an off-season mini-camp, Howe failed to show up on the second day. The Rangers tracked him down in Waco, where he was shacked up with a dancer from Lace, the same east Arlington strip club where Billy Martin, then with the Yankees, had been beaten up a few years earlier.

The Rangers' brass had taken a hotel suite at the Marriott near the stadium and were peering out the window when Howe rolled up in the passenger seat of a convertible, shirtless and, according to Valentine in his autobiography, smoking dope.

Valentine wrote: "Mike Stone opened the door [to the hotel room where the Rangers' brass waited], and Howe walked in with a tattered T-shirt, glazed eyes and a shit-eating grin on his face. 'Don't have me pee in that jar for a while,' Steve said."

Valentine said he leaped over a couch in the room, grabbed Howe by his T-shirt and pushed him up hard against the sliding-glass door that led to the patio before gaining control of his temper.

Valentine's memory of the details may be shaded with a bit of hyperbole — Rangers drug counselor Sam McDowell, not Stone, was in the room with Grieve, and neither McDowell nor Grieve recalls anyone getting physical — but the ass-chewing that Valentine proceeded to give Howe, Grieve said, was Lasorda-esque in its eloquence, its creativity and its virulence.

Mostly though, Valentine blamed himself. He'd stuck his neck out for Howe and been burned, badly. It would cost the Rangers a quarter of a million dollars.

Howe would fail in the major leagues one last time, with the Yankees. He died when he crashed his truck in the California desert in 2006. He was 48 years old.

Valentine, in his win-now mode, was also among those who pushed hard for the disastrous 1989 trade that sent Sammy Sosa, Scott Fletcher and Wilson Álvarez to the White Sox for outfielder/DH Harold Baines. With right-handed hitters Julio Franco, Pete Incaviglia and Steve Buechele in place, Valentine felt he needed another left-handed RBI bat to complement Rafael Palmeiro and switch-hitting Ruben Sierra. And he had unanimous support from the Rangers' front office to make the trade.

But Baines, a Chicago icon who had practically made a career out of hammering Rangers' pitching, was so devastated by the trade that he was barely a shell of himself in Texas. He was miserable, and so was his performance. It was one of the most disappointing outcomes to a deal in Rangers history.

~ ~ ~

WHEN I THINK back on Valentine's seven seasons in Texas, it's not the controversies he stirred up with his mouth, nor his run-ins with umpires, nor his over-the-top hyperbole that stands out. It was his incredible energy, his dogged determination not just to turn his young players into big-leaguers, but to reconstruct an entire community into a major-league destination.

That's what he accomplished in Texas. He didn't win a championship or take his team to the playoffs — he would do that in his next stop with the New York Mets — but under his watch the Rangers finally grew up. Texas, at long last, became a real major-league franchise.

After the 1985 season, the *Star-Telegram* flew me to New York the week after Christmas to do a profile on Valentine. My wife and I took the train out of Penn Station to his hometown of Stamford, Conn., where we met up in his first restaurant. Behind the bar they were showing old video clips of young Bobby as a football star at Rippowam High, where he was the first three-time All-Stater in Connecticut history.

The kid was a touchdown machine. He made All-State four times in baseball and was recruited heavily by USC, Notre Dame and dozens of other colleges.

But this athletic prodigy had also been a finalist in International Ballroom Dancing competitions and performed with his partner at the 1964 World's Fair. To say that Valentine was Stamford's favorite son in those days would be a vast understatement.

On New Year's Eve, we joined Valentine and his wife Mary to celebrate at one of his other nearby restaurants that was featuring a live band. Valentine was showing off some of his dance moves when a pained look suddenly crossed his face. His shoulder had popped out of place.

"Don't worry," he told us, forcing a smile. "Happens all the time."

He manipulated the injured shoulder, popped it back into place and went back to dancing.

Life was always a dance to Bobby Valentine. He loved the rhythm of it, the beat, the melody. Sometimes no one else could hear the music — but he could, and that was all that mattered.

Chapter 10

THE RYAN EXPRESS
Signing a Superhero

Nolan Ryan, meeting the media with manager Bobby Valentine in December 1988, shocked the baseball world when he signed with the Rangers during the winter meetings.

NOLAN RYAN'S *arrival as a free agent in 1989 was the most im-pactful event in Texas Rangers history since the David Clyde game 26 years earlier.*

Ryan's presence gave the franchise credibility and a sense of gravitas that had been sorely missing. It also changed the attitude of both the Rangers players and the employees in the front office. They began to believe in the future again.

IT IS A BEAUTIFUL spring day in Port Charlotte, Fla., and Nolan Ryan and I have just departed the Texas Rangers' spring-training camp in his rental car, heading west on Florida's State Highway 776, a 25-mile-long loop that extends about a dozen miles to Englewood Beach on the Gulf of Mexico, before turning back east into southern Sarasota County.

It is still early in camp in the spring of 1990. Games haven't begun yet, but pitchers and catchers have reported, and Ryan, whose workout regimen is legendary, is preparing for his second season as a Ranger at the age of 43. Ryan is aging not so much like fine wine as like a prime porterhouse steak — a much more appropriate metaphor, since he has been entrenched in the beef business for years.

On this particular day, after his workout, Ryan had methodically worked through his daily autograph session in the "Nolan Ryan State Pen," a chain-link enclosure erected in the parking lot behind the Rangers clubhouse to corral the crowds lining up to have something signed by the fabled right-hander. As usual, more than a hundred fans had queued up for autographs after practice, including several "professional" autograph collectors who showed up daily to score signed items to list on eBay.

Ryan has no problem signing for fans, but he views the professional autograph hounds as if they were cockroaches that just wriggled out of his cheeseburger. His amiable good-ol'-boy attitude can disappear in a flash, to be replaced by the Ryan who would have no problem sizzling a 98-mph fastball in the vicinity of a batter's chin.

So he has established a policy of signing just one item for each person. Occasionally a collector might attempt to circle through the line more than once, sometimes even changing shirts to alter his or her appearance. Big mistake. Ryan has an eagle eye for such offenders. Those caught attempting this tactic not only get an ear-burning lecture from Ryan but risk being banished from future autograph sessions.

Autograph collectors, even well-meaning ones, can be amazingly insensitive to the players' need for privacy. They see a famous figure like Ryan having lunch in a restaurant and they can't resist coming over.

"Mr. Ryan, I hate to bother you," they start out, and Ryan mutters under his breath, "But you will anyway." They continue, "I wonder if

you would mind signing my ... [menu, baseball glove, arm, wife]."
Ryan is still bemused by one fan with a broken ankle who propped his
foot on Ryan's table alongside the legend's grilled chicken breast and
asked him to sign his cast.

"Man, you need to wash your toes!" Ryan exclaimed. But he
signed anyway. He always does.

On this spring day, we're headed to lunch in Port Charlotte, so
I'm confused when Nolan swings the car west out of the team's training facility instead of east toward town. Nolan keeps glancing in his
rearview mirror at a car following close behind us.

In a few minutes the future Hall of Famer pulls off onto a side
street in El Jobean, a tiny fishing village on the banks of the Mayakka
River. The sedan behind us turns in, too. Ryan pulls sharply into a
cul-de-sac. He instructs me to stay put, then gets out and marches
purposefully back to the vehicle that has pulled up 15 yards behind
us.

The driver in the car is looking decidedly uncomfortable as Ryan,
clearly unhappy, approaches. The big Texan leans into the driver's
open window and waves a finger in the man's face. I can't quite make
out what Ryan is saying, but I'm pretty sure it's not going to be print-
able in the family newspaper I work for back in Fort Worth, Texas.

Is the guy in the car going to leap out brandishing a pistol? Will
there be fisticuffs? At this point, the famous noogie-thrashing Ryan
was to give young rookie Robin Ventura is still three years down the
road, but it couldn't be clearer to me that Ryan isn't inclined to put up
with any nonsense. Do I need to call for back-up? *Am I supposed to
be the back-up?*

Never mind. Ryan is striding back to the car. The driver in the
sedan, properly chastised, has put his vehicle in reverse and is pulling away. His plan of following us to lunch to collect yet another autograph has been thoroughly quashed. I breathe a sigh of relief. No
blood, no foul.

One more strikeout for the living legend.

~ ~ ~

MORE THAN 30 years later, lunch with Nolan Ryan hasn't changed
much. I could be dining with a cousin in Nacogdoches, or maybe an
old friend in San Angelo, instead of with one of the most recognizable
Texas icons ever. He's still that humble, that down-to-earth.

And the Ryan family is still involved with baseball, through its part-ownership of the Rangers' Triple-A affiliate, the Round Rock Express. Ryan's elder son, Reid, is CEO of Ryan-Sanders Baseball (Sanders is Houston financier and former Astros minority owner Don Sanders).

So today we're lunching in the Central Texas city of Round Rock, just down the street from Ryan's office in the R Bank, which in turn is only a couple of blocks from Dell Diamond, home of the Round Rock Express.

Ryan's younger son, Reese, has joined us at the restaurant. He's 46 now, but I remember him at 14, getting his dad's massive front-loader tractor stuck in the mud while we were deer-hunting on one of the Ryan ranches in deep south Texas the week after Christmas one year. Now he's chairman of the board for R Bank and Ryan Brands.

Between the charred-vegetable appetizer and the Irish stew (with Nolan Ryan Angus Beef, naturally), the three of us talk about baseball, Ryan's life — he and his wife, Ruth, now live in Georgetown, just up I-35 from Round Rock — and the documentary the family has persuaded him to participate in. He wasn't keen on doing the documentary at first, but he relented when Ruth and his grown children — Reid, Reese and Wendy — argued that it would be a gift to his grandchildren, a chance for them to better understand just who their Pawpaw is and why everyone seems to know him.

"Reid told me I'd only have to do a couple of sit-down interviews for it," he says, shaking his head. "I think I did about 15." The documentary, with interviews from teammates and players spanning his 27-year career, has been debuted at Austin's South by Southwest festival to critical acclaim. Ryan and both sons are listed among the executive producers.

Ryan's voice still sounds like home, his Texas drawl as soothing as a hot biscuit with butter oozing down its sides at sunrise. It's like being in the middle of an Olshan TV commercial without the foundation problems. Just listening, I realize how much I've missed being around this sensible, decent man over the last three decades.

Unless he's visiting one of his ranches or traveling on company business, the 75-year-old Ryan is in his office every day. He seems a little shocked when Reese points out that it has been nearly 30 years since he retired from playing after the 1993 season.

Ryan is sporting a new left knee, after replacement surgery a few years ago. There's the horseshoe-shaped scar on his right cheek where years of sun-drenched spring trainings and long, hot days on the ranch exacted their price, a scary melanoma removed three years ago.

"You know," he drawls, "we never thought about using sunscreen in those days. I sure do now, though."

～ ～ ～

IN 1988, Ryan shocked the baseball world by signing a free-agent contract with the Texas Rangers at the Winter Meetings in Atlanta. It was a one-year deal with a club option for a second year, but Ryan, 42 at the time, figured he likely had only one season left anyway. After that, it would be off to tend full time to his cattle and his thriving beef business.

Except … there was still five more years of greatness in that right arm.

Ryan had given the Houston Astros everything he had for nine seasons. But Astros owner John McMullen never made a pitch to keep him. Instead, the Astros offered him an insulting 20 percent cut in pay. Other teams, meanwhile, were crossing their fingers and hoping he would look their way.

It came down to three clubs: the Angels, the Giants and the Rangers, who had asked to make their pitch last.

Ryan had close relationships with major figures on all three teams: owner Gene Autry with the Angels, general manager Al Rosen with the Giants, manager Bobby Valentine with the Rangers. It was the Angels that made the first solid offer. Then the Giants got serious with an offer. Meanwhile, the Rangers were lying in the weeds, waiting for their chance.

The Rangers had a built-in advantage, something the others simply couldn't match: the state of Texas. Ryan, a born-and-bred Texan, owned three working cattle ranches in the state. Playing for the Astros, he'd been able to live in Alvin, the Texas town near Houston where he grew up. Being close to his family and ranches was critical to him.

Crusty Rangers owner Eddie Chiles should have gotten much more credit than he did for signing off on the team's pursuit of Ryan. With the oil business cratering and his Western Co. feeling the crunch, Chiles was in dire straits financially. But he told club president Mike Stone and general manager Tom Grieve to let him worry about the money — just sign Ryan if they could.

And the Rangers' Valentine — who'd been in center field for the Angels when Ryan threw his third no-hitter — made sure Nolan and Ruth understood that Ryan's teen-age sons would be welcome around the team. As I mentioned earlier, the Astros' policy of barring players' kids in the clubhouse or on the field grated on the Ryans.

With the Rangers, Valentine told them, the boys could hang out in the clubhouse, take batting practice in the indoor cage, shag fly balls in the outfield, even travel on team charter flights if they wanted. Ryan could even occasionally scoot back to Alvin on weekends when the team was home and he wasn't scheduled to pitch.

It was exactly what Nolan and Ruth wanted to hear.

~ ~ ~

IT WOULD be impossible to overstate the impact Ryan's signing had on the Rangers franchise.

Besides his still-blazing fastball and his knee-buckling curveball, Ryan brought instant credibility to the Rangers. He gave the franchise the kind of national stature and respect from other teams it had never enjoyed before. He was the Rangers' first and still greatest superhero.

Even better, as far as the fans were concerned, he was as Texan as a pair of scuffed-up cowboy boots and a sweat-stained Stetson hat. He gave Texas fans something to be proud of while they were waiting for the team to finally win something. And no one, including Ryan himself, had anticipated just how good he would be.

The 1989 season with the Rangers would be Ryan's 22nd full season. He was just 225 strikeouts shy of 5,000, but after nine seasons pitching in the air-conditioned Astrodome for Houston, he wasn't sure if he could handle working outdoors during a Texas summer in Arlington Stadium. That was his major concern as he headed north up Interstate 45.

Maybe growing up in Texas had already acclimated him to the heat, because it didn't seem to bother him at all. Nothing seemed to faze him — not heat, not age, not even taking a Bo Jackson one-hopper off his kisser a few years later.

That last incident was memorialized in an iconic photo of Ryan continuing to pitch with blood streaming from his busted lip and splattered on his white Rangers jersey. I have a copy autographed by Ryan hanging on the wall in my office, a gift from Tom Vandergriff's grandson Parker.

One of my most vivid memories of covering Ryan is watching his legendary spring-training conditioning routine. Juggling the demands of baseball and his cattle business, he would often show up at camp a week behind the other pitchers (with permission from the club, of course). Then, on his first day in camp, he would throw four or five innings of batting practice, far more than any other pitcher in camp.

Throughout the spring, sitting in the press box at Charlotte County Stadium, the Texas beat writers could look over the right-field fence and watch Ryan taking the outdoor stairs on the team's two-story office building two steps at a time. Up and down, up and down, over and over again. It was as if he had reversed the numbers on his age and was only 24.

The work paid off when the season started. Six times in that first season with the Rangers he lost potential no-hitters in the seventh inning or later. Twice he took no-hitters into the ninth, two more into the eighth. Each time he walked away disappointed, thinking it might be the last time he would be that close.

"I thought that part of my life was probably over with," Ryan conceded at the time.

It had been eight years since Ryan had broken Sandy Koufax's no-hitter record, on Sept. 26, 1981, pitching for the Astros against the Los Angeles Dodgers. With the Rangers out of contention, I had been at the Astrodome that afternoon to cover the Astros-Dodgers pennant battle.

The funny things you remember from the days that history is made: That day in 1981 when Ryan pitched his fifth no-hitter, I recall that he had worn a hole in the sanitary sock on his right foot from pushing off the mound, and his big toe was sticking out as he told the crowd of reporters surrounding him that he didn't compare himself to Koufax.

"I saw him pitch as a kid, and he was the most overpowering pitcher with control that I've ever seen play the game," Ryan had said. "I'm sure he's the greatest left-hander of all time."

And I remember Ryan, who had tied Koufax's record of four no-hitters six years earlier, saying afterward that he hadn't been sure he had the stamina to finish off a fifth no-hitter at his age. He was 34 at the time.

"I had really started to wonder if I'd ever get it," he'd said then. "I was starting to wonder if it was in the books for me."

Oh, it was in the books, along with several more historic chapters.

In his seasons with the Rangers, Ryan would give the Astros' Mc-Mullen plenty of opportunities to rue his lowball offer. Among the things that Houston missed by letting Ryan slip away:

Aug. 22, 1989: Strikeout No. 5,000.

June 11, 1990: Ryan's sixth no-hitter, in Oakland.

July 31, 1990: Win No. 300, in Milwaukee.

May 1, 1991: No-hitter *No. 7,* vs. Toronto in Arlington.

THESE WERE all phenomenal accomplishments, particularly given Ryan's age. But all would be eclipsed in entertainment value by the event that happened on the night of Aug. 4, 1993, when 26-year-old Robin Ventura decided to charge the mound on the John Wayne of baseball.

You just don't do that, pilgrim.

"All these years, that's the first question that comes up," he says as we sip our iced tea after lunch. "I always say, of all the things I accomplished in my career, it's funny how that's what people think about. I understand that mindset, though."

It was the culmination of a feud that had been brewing between the Chicago White Sox and the Texas Rangers for three years, since the spring of 1990, when Chicago's Lilliputian utility infielder Craig Grebeck hit a home run off Ryan in an exhibition game. The little infielder may have admired it a tad too long for Ryan's taste — although, looking at it from Grebeck's perspective, it was probably the highlight of his career at the time.

When the regular season began and the diminutive Grebeck astonishingly did it again at Comiskey Park — skipping around the bases like a kid with a brand-new lollipop — the gloves came off.

"Who is that boy?" Ryan grumpily asked pitching coach Tom House once he was back in the dugout between innings. "He looks like he's about 12." Both agreed that Grebeck was having way too much fun.

A week later Ryan buried a fastball in "that boy's" ribs, and the beanball war was on. It would rise and wane over the next three seasons, until that fateful night in early August 1993 at Arlington Stadium when Ventura stepped to the plate.

If you haven't seen the video by now, or heard the story, welcome back to civilization; you have a lot of catching up to do. Movies are in color now, too.

The carnage that piled up in the first game of the three-game series might have tipped us off that a boiling point was at hand. It started in the second inning of Game 1 with Rangers right-hander Roger Pavlik's pitch nailing White Sox catcher Ron Karkovice. In the bottom of the inning, White Sox starter Jason Bere evened the score by clipping Rangers third baseman Dean Palmer; in the sixth, Chicago reliever Bobby Thigpen came in wild and hit both Palmer and infielder Mario Diaz.

The next day, with tempers simmering, both teams showed up expecting trouble.

"We've heard that the White Sox players had decided among themselves that the next batter hit by a Rangers pitcher would go to the mound," Reese Ryan tells me at our lunch in Round Rock.

Any hitter who failed to retaliate against the offending pitcher would catch hell at the team's next Kangaroo Court, a time-honored MLB tradition of peer justice in which players enforce mostly unwritten rules among themselves without resorting to the front office. There would a fine and public ridicule, along with pointed questions about the hitter's manhood.

It was a Rangers batter who took the first hit when White Sox left-hander Sid Fernandez drilled Juan Gonzalez leading off the second inning. Anyone else sensing a trend here?

Designated hitter Matt Merullo led off the Chicago third, and Ryan disposed of him quickly on a first-pitch pop fly to center. With one out, Ventura settled into the left-hand batter's box.

Ryan had hit a dozen batters the season before, but he had yet to plunk a single one in '93. That was about to change.

Ventura was a quiet, reserved player with a reputation as a nice guy, the kind who called his elders "sir" and "ma'am." The 46-year-old Ryan certainly had nothing against the former Oklahoma State star personally. They'd never even met. But in the first inning, Ventura had reached across the plate to line a fastball to left center, plating the game's first run. Diving across the plate to reach outside pitches was a favored tactic among White Sox hitters. It was a technique taught by White Sox hitting coach Walt Hriniak, who believed in hitting the ball the opposite way.

Ryan, who believed all 17 inches of the plate belonged to him, didn't appreciate the strategy.

When Ventura stepped in with his wide-open stance, well off the plate, there was no hesitation on Ryan's part. Firmly believing that the best way to prevent hitters from diving across the plate was to own the inside corner, Ryan fired off his first pitch to Ventura. It was, in the famous words of Bob Uecker in the movie "Major League," "just a tad inside."

There are those who argue that the pitch wasn't *that* far inside. They need to take another look at the video. If Ventura hadn't twisted away from the pitch, it would have hit him squarely on the numeral 3 of his No. 23 jersey instead of his right shoulder blade. It was *way* inside.

Was Ryan a headhunter? Did he hit Ventura on purpose? The statistics themselves answer the first question. In more than 5,300 innings pitched over 27 years, Ryan hit 158 batters, placing him 15th on the list of HBP (hit by pitch). Do the math: Ryan averaged not quite six batters hit per season. For a guy who led the league in walks eight times and in strikeouts 11 times, that's not bad at all. Other pitchers did far more damage with far fewer opportunities.

Not even once in almost 35 years did I ever hear Ryan admit to hitting a batter on purpose. He's too smart for that. What he does say, repeatedly, is that pitching inside is part of the game, especially *his* game, which absolutely included intimidation.

Ventura clearly wasn't enthusiastic about charging an icon like Ryan. If he had kicked the living daylights out of a man 20 years his senior, a national hero with 52 major-league pitching records on his resume, what would he have accomplished beyond making himself the most hated man in baseball history, a national pariah? Would he have even escaped Arlington without being torn to pieces? And if he had, would he have ever been safe crossing the state line again?

After the pitch connected, Ventura hesitated, not once but twice. His first instinct was simply to head to first base. Head down, as the realization of what had just happened settled in, he took a couple of steps toward first.

Then it suddenly dawned on him: He'd been hit; the machismo of baseball demanded that he stand up for himself and his team by confronting his attacker. He threw down his bat and his helmet and

Nolan Ryan took charge when Robin Ventura charged the mound after Ryan tried to claim home plate with an inside pitch in 1993. "I always say, of all the things I accomplished in my career, it's funny how that's what people think about."

rushed toward Ryan, who met him with a question.

"What are you doing out here?"

Ventura's charge slowed. It was as if he was asking himself, "Good question: What *am* I doing out here?"

Ryan, on the other hand, had planned for this exact scenario for years. Thirteen years to the day, in fact.

On Aug. 3, 1980, while pitching for the Astros, Ryan had unleashed three straight "purpose" pitches in the general direction of San Diego Padres outfielder Dave Winfield. None connected, but it wasn't because Ryan wasn't trying. They were too close for Winfield, who had grown tired of playing Twister to avoid Ryan's fastballs. The enraged 6-foot-6, 230-pound Winfield flicked away both Astros catcher Alan Ashby and home plate umpire Lanny Harris as if they were bothersome gnats and was on top of Ryan in three giant strides. He unleashed a right hand that just missed crushing Ryan's skull.

"It was one of those big roundhouse swings," Ryan tells me. "I ducked it, and by then everybody and their dog was on top of me. If he had connected, he could have hurt me. I made up my mind after that that I wouldn't be passive the next time someone came to the mound. I would do what I had to do to protect myself."

In Ryan's mind, that meant taking charge, and Ventura's hesitation played right into that. As Ventura ducked into him, Ryan threw a left arm around his neck, tucked the younger man's head under that arm, and rode him like a steer wrestler.

It was Noogie Time in Texas.

We all know the rest of the story: how players piled on until Ryan and Ventura were eventually dragged down under the weight of dozens of bodies; how Ryan was crushed beneath the pile, unable to catch his breath until Chicago strong man Bo Jackson began throwing players from both teams aside and pulled Ryan to his feet.

"I couldn't breathe. I thought for a minute there that I was gonna die," Ryan admits to me at the restaurant in Round Rock, contemplating his empty stew bowl. One look at his face tells me he's not exaggerating. He was so grateful to Jackson that after the game he phoned him to thank him again.

Ryan gets no pleasure out of the realization that, after all he accomplished in the game — the seven no-hitters, the record-setting 5,714 strikeouts, the 324 victories, the 52 pitching records he still holds — what he is most known for today is applying five or six noogies and one good uppercut to the face of a nice kid like Robin Ventura.

There was never any real animosity between the two, not then and not now.

"What I did when he got the manager's job with the White Sox [in 2012], his first game managing was Opening Day at Arlington," says Ryan, who was club president at the time. "I went over there about 30 minutes before the game to congratulate him on getting the job. I told him I was sorry that thing had taken on a life of its own. He was fine with it. It was pretty much out of character for him."

It had been 19 years since the incident, and they'd never talked about it until then.

~ ~ ~

THE VENTURA brawl aside, Ryan has mostly good memories of his time in Texas, especially as a player, but also during the six years he spent as club president and CEO, from 2008 to 2013. Why wouldn't he? Under his guidance, the Rangers made their first two trips to the World Series in 2010 and 2011.

"One pitch, twice," he says, shaking his head, "and we didn't get it done."

As every Rangers fan painfully knows, that's how close Texas was to winning it all against St. Louis in 2011. Instead, the Cardinals rallied to win Game 6, then captured Game 7 to send the Rangers reeling home in disappointment.

It didn't end well for the Rangers then, and it didn't end well for Ryan, who elected to step down as CEO after the 2013 season. He'd been stripped of his baseball operations authority by owner Ray Davis a year earlier.

"I wasn't prepared for that job when I took it," Ryan concedes now. "I'd never run a company before like that. I look back on things that I definitely would have changed."

Summing up his tenure as CEO, he says: "I gave everybody a chance to keep their jobs and to do the job."

As usual, he's being modest. He changed the franchise's culture, building a front office that felt like family. There's a reason he was given a standing ovation by the employees the first day he walked into the Rangers offices after he and Chuck Greenberg won the rights in court to purchase the franchise for $385 million in August of 2010.

Otherwise, though, he says he wouldn't change a thing about his Rangers experience, both on the field and in the front office.

"Some things happened that were pretty momentous," he says. "I didn't go there thinking I would get 5,000 strikeouts. I didn't go there thinking about winning 300 games. I certainly didn't think about the no-hitters."

Nor did he ever dream he might someday become part-owner, club president or CEO, or that he would take the Texas Rangers to the brink of a World Series championship. He came to Arlington hoping for one more year of doing what he loved; instead, he became a legend.

Walking out of the restaurant, we pass three young men who are just arriving. One of them can't resist. He turns back, catches up to us and says, "Mr. Ryan?"

Nolan Ryan stops and turns around.

"Mr. Ryan," the young man says, "I just want to shake your hand and thank you for everything you've done."

I get the feeling he's speaking for the whole state of Texas.

Chapter 11

THE TURNING POINT
A Bush and a Ballpark

B ALLPARK *IS A WORD exclusive to baseball. No one calls a football stadium a "ballpark." Same with soccer, or rugby, or whatever
game you're playing on the grass.*

Ballpark equals baseball. Period.

*When the Texas Rangers finally left their first home — Arlington
Stadium, decrepit but still beloved by some, myself included — to move
a few hundred yards south in 1994, they moved into The Ballpark in
Arlington, with all the connotations that cherished word means to the
souls of baseball fans everywhere.*

*Now THIS was a ballpark, replete with the latest innovations but
wrapped in a comforting retro quilt of nostalgia. From the soaring
Home Run Porch to the spacious open galleries encircling the park to
the Lone Star symbols above the arches, The Ballpark in Arlington was
a TEXAS ballpark.*

It made a statement: Baseball *would be played here, Texas-style.*

*The journey to that uniquely Texan stadium, however, was a circu-
itous one that could have been derailed at any number of points along
the way. It was a journey that involved, among other things, a future
president.*

SOME WILL CONTEND that the most pivotal moment in Texas
Rangers history occurred on Oct. 22, 2010, when a slider from Nef-
tali Feliz froze Alex Rodriguez to send the Rangers to their first-ever
World Series.

I understand that thinking. Just the fact that it was A-Rod made
it deliciously symbolic. As far as a single moment in time, nothing
could beat that instant when we realized that the Rangers were going
to be one of the last two teams playing in October. It was the dream

come true, the one we had cherished for more than three decades.

But was it the most important event in Rangers history? As powerful a moment as the Feliz strikeout was, I would argue that nothing changed the fortunes and future of the Texas Rangers more than the day in 1994 when they cut the ribbon on The Ballpark in Arlington.

That's when the Texas Rangers became major-league. Without The Ballpark in Arlington, I can't imagine that incredibly momentous strikeout in October 2010 could ever have happened.

Can anyone picture that glorious moment taking place in Arlington Stadium, bless its pea-pickin' heart?

Yeah, me neither.

The Ballpark in Arlington: The Home Run Porch. The Jumbotrons in left field and above the Porch roof. The balconies on the office building in center field. Greene's Hill. THIS was a ballpark!

Its beauty captured the heart, but there was a much more practical benefit that came with The Ballpark in Arlington — increased revenue.

With the revenue from the old park, "it was obvious that we would not be able to compete," noted longtime color analyst and former player and general manager Tom Grieve. "The increased revenue from better seating, the suites, put us on a level playing field. Without that new stadium, we wouldn't have had the revenue to support a team that could be in the playoffs or World Series."

To trace the origins of the success the Rangers would ultimately discover in the 2000s, we must go back even further, to the end of the 1980s and the close of Fort Worth oilman Eddie Chiles' reign.

Chiles was the third owner in Rangers history, after Bob Short and Brad Corbett, and every one of them was a maverick. They shot from the hip and worried about the bloodstains later. It was an approach that was often entertaining but seldom conducive to long-term success.

Chiles had built his fortune with an oil drilling company he had started back in 1939 that eventually evolved into the Western Company of North America. He was not a baseball man; in fact, his favorite thing in the world, next to making money, was University of Oklahoma football. But, when Corbett's group ran short of money in 1980, Chiles had seen keeping Rangers ownership local as something of a civic duty, so he stepped in.

Almost a decade later, it was Chiles who was looking for a bailout as the oil business collapsed around him. He put the Rangers up for sale.

His decision caused panic at Arlington City Hall. It was 1988, and Richard Greene was in his second year as mayor of Arlington when Chiles called him and told him he was moving forward to "defease the bonds."

Greene wasn't sure what that meant, but he found out when he called former mayor Tom Vandergriff — who "uncharacteristically responded with alarm."

"The bonds in question were the remaining debts on Arlington Stadium that had been built up over the years of adding seating, suites, press facilities, etc., to try and bring the facility up closer to major-league standards," Greene explained to me in an interview for this book.

For $1 million, Chiles had bought the option to acquire Arlington Stadium, its parking rights, concessions and broadcast rights after Vandergriff left office. Mayor S.J. Stovall's city council had sold that option to Chiles to help them defray the crushing debt the city faced from the ill-fated Seven Seas marine park, Greene explained: The city's credit rating was at stake.

But now, Greene said, the city was faced with the prospect that Chiles would pay off the outstanding bonds to gain title to the stadium property, then unload the 100-plus acres "to some real estate developer who would see all that property as prime land of I-30 frontage development."

If that happened, any new owners "would be looking to Dallas," Greene explained, "as just about everyone anywhere had already concluded that only Dallas would have the financial capacity to build a new ballpark."

"The result, Vandergriff feared: Arlington was going to lose the Rangers," Greene told me.

"It's hard to explain the pain in his voice on that phone call," Greene recalls. "I assured him that would never happen. It became my priority to deliver on that promise."

Eventually, Greene was able to fulfill his promise, but in the end it would take a canny real estate deal and a hotly contested bond campaign for a higher sales tax to keep the Rangers in Arlington.

~ ~ ~

MEANWHILE, potential buyers for the franchise had already begun popping out of the woodwork.

So had I, in a manner of speaking. After covering the Rangers as a beat man for the *Fort Worth Star-Telegram* for a dozen years, from the mid-'70s to the mid-'80s, I had morphed into a general sports columnist with an emphasis on the Rangers. When Chiles put the team on the market in 1986, I was asked by sports editor Bruce Raben to take on the coverage of the sale as a special assignment. No one knew then that the process would drag on for almost three years.

The assignment was challenging and exhilarating. It was also a something of a turning point in my career. After it was over, and the Rangers were under the control of the son of the president of the United States, I was nominated for a Pulitzer Prize by the *Star-Telegram* for my cumulative coverage of the sale. It was a journalistic milestone in my career, and I was honored and humbled.

I also knew I owed most of the credit to a man you've likely never heard of — a real estate broker named Dan Shackelford. After leaving IBM and moving to Arlington, Shackelford and two partners had opened a real estate office. A former college baseball player, Shackelford still had a love for the game. He was a neighbor of Rangers bullpen coach Larry Hardy, knew club president Mike Stone and relished

Eddie and Fran Chiles, center, agreed to sell the Texas Rangers baseball team to a group fronted by George W. Bush, second from right, and his partner Edward "Rusty" Rose, far left, in 1989.

these slight connections to the team. (Eventually, in fact, Dan would suffer a major stroke while visiting Hardy during spring training in Port Charlotte, Fla.)

"Shack" would become my Deep Throat, a la Woodward and Bernstein. All that was missing was a darkened underground parking garage and a mysterious figure in a trench coat.

Early on I had learned that Shackelford was part of a group interested in buying the Rangers. I never heard who the money man or men were in his group, but I figured out that his main interest was in brokering a deal in which the new owners of the club would build a ballpark on a piece of property he was connected to near the intersection of I-30 and Loop 12.

Shackelford did not, under any circumstances, want his name in the newspaper. He never explained exactly why, but he was adamant about it. I told him I couldn't promise that. Then he made me an offer I couldn't refuse.

The deal we struck was this: If I would keep his name out of my stories, he would provide me inside information on what was going on with the sale, which group had just come in, who was a serious contender, who was likely dropping out. Knowing the decision to go along was above my pay grade, I called my editor from Shackelford's office to run the deal by him. Raben spoke briefly to Shackelford himself and signed off on our arrangement.

It wasn't Watergate, but our Deep Throat came through like gangbusters. We didn't meet in subterranean parking garages or send coded messages; almost-daily phone calls were good enough. Shackelford's tips were pure gold. When a new group would show up with an offer, he would let me know. I was breaking stories on the sale on a regular basis.

When former Rangers marketing vice president Larry Schmittou came in representing a Nashville group, I had the scoop. When team president Mike Stone got involved with a local group of prospective buyers, I broke the story first. Same with Parker County car dealer Roger Williams, whose partners would have included Fort Worth's Tom Schieffer, who would come back into the picture later, and real estate developer Mike Reilly.

Though he never admitted it, I suspected Shackelford was somehow connected to Chicago White Sox owner Jerry Reinsdorf. Reinsdorf was chairman of the MLB's Ownership Committee, the group that approved or disapproved new ownership. Shackelford was likely getting his information straight from the horse's mouth.

The day he first whispered that the son of the president was a major player, the front man for a group that had baseball commissioner Peter Ueberroth's blessing, I almost did a backflip. Now, this was *news!*

~ ~ ~

THE FIRST TIME George W. Bush and I spoke on the phone, shortly after he was announced as co-managing partner of the Rangers, he lectured me on ground rules for how our relationship was going to work.

"You are NOT getting my home phone number," Bush said emphatically. This told me a couple of things about him. The first, of course, was that the rules regarding official protocol for the son of the president were not to be bent, disregarded or trifled with under any circumstances. The second was that he'd done his homework. He knew something about me.

Not having given much thought to Secret Service concerns, I'd already been whining to Rangers PR guru John Blake about the prospect of not having Bush's home number. I'd had home numbers for Brad Corbett and Eddie Chiles for years, and many of those calls, especially those late-night chats after the owners might have had a few nightcaps, had resulted in breaking news stories and spectacular headlines, such as when Corbett declared he might just "sell the Rangers to a bunch of Arabs!"

Bush was letting me know that those days were at an end. I would have to work through Blake when I needed to talk to the new managing partner. To his credit, I can't remember a time when Bush didn't get back to me after I'd made that call to Blake.

When Bush and his investors came into the Rangers' ownership picture, Ueberroth knew he had his man. This was high-profile stuff. Only one problem: Bush's group lacked sufficient local ownership. DFW was a top-10 market, and Ueberroth was determined that Major League Baseball should be entrenched there.

The Rangers' sale process had already gone off the rails. Chiles had initially agreed to sell the team to Florida car dealer and philanthropist Frank Morsani, whose thinly veiled plan was to move the franchise to his home city of Tampa. Everybody but Chiles seemed to know about Morsani's agenda.

Once Chiles realized his blunder — local media and citizenry were practically lighting torches and sharpening pitchforks to march on Chiles' ivory tower at the Western Co. — he begged minority partner Eddie Gaylord to bail him out of the Morsani sale by exercising his right of first refusal.

Gaylord did, shutting down the Morsani threat, but then he ran into issues of his own. A media mogul who owned DFW station KTVT-TV, Gaylord had intended to turn Channel 11 into a superstation like Atlanta's TBS or Chicago's WGN, with Texas Rangers games being broadcast into homes nationwide just like the Braves or Cubs were. Major League Baseball did not want another superstation. It rejected Gaylord's bid.

At that point Cincinnati sports investor Bill DeWitt Jr. made a phone call.

DeWitt had a long history with baseball. His dad, Bill DeWitt Sr., had once owned the St. Louis Browns and the Cincinnati Reds; DeWitt Jr. had been the 9-year-old batboy whose uniform 3-foot-7-inch player Eddie Gaedel wore when Browns owner Bill Veeck sent him up to pinch-hit at Sportsman's Park as a publicity stunt.

DeWitt had also done some business with George W. Bush in the Permian Basin with an oil company named Spectrum 7, and the two had remained friendly. DeWitt knew George W. was a huge baseball fan and was looking for some way to distinguish himself from his father after a failed run for Congress.

Now DeWitt phoned his friend George W. with an intriguing message: "The Rangers are back in play."

Bush's original ownership group included his cousin by marriage, Connecticut real estate magnate Craig Stapleton, and former Marriott and Northwest Airlines exec Fred Malek, a D.C.-area wheeler-dealer who had been a member of Nixon's inner circle and served in various posts in his administration. DeWitt Jr. was part of a Cincinnati contingent with oilman and investor Mercer Reynolds, media executive Dudley S. Taft Sr. and produce wholesaler Bob Castellini (now the current owner of the Cincinnati Reds). Bush also had recruited friends Roland Betts and Tom Bernstein out of New York.

But Ueberroth told Bush he needed more local ownership. Bush, in turn, approached well-known Fort Worth investment specialist

Richard Rainwater on at least two occasions, only to be turned down. Finally, Ueberroth made his own pitch directly to Rainwater.

"Ueberroth convinced Rainwater this wasn't a vanity thing; he could make money on it," recalled Tom Schieffer, who was also in the mix as a local prospect for the Bush group. "Rainwater finally agreed, but he said, 'I don't want to own the team outright.' He agreed to invest 10 percent on the condition that he could bring in Rusty Rose [owner of Cardinal Investments in Dallas] to be his numbers guy."

Rose had acquired the rather gloomy nickname "The Mortician" for his skill at squeezing profits from failing companies through leveraged buyouts. It was agreed that Bush — despite the relative insignificance of his initial investment — would be the managing partner and front man, dealing with the media and the public. Rose, the introvert, would be chairman of the board.

"Rusty had suffered through a bout of serious depression" — it would eventually take his life, years later — "and Richard told him, 'You need to do this because you need to do something fun,'" recalled Schieffer.

For his part, Fort Worth native Schieffer could hardly have been more local. The younger brother of CBS-TV journalist Bob Schieffer, he grew up in Fort Worth's River Oaks neighborhood and attended the city's Arlington Heights High School. Successful in both law and business and civically active in Fort Worth, Schieffer was approached by Bush's people after they had obtained a letter of intent to sell from Chiles.

Having served several terms in the Texas Legislature, he reminded them that he was a stalwart Democrat. He'd voted for Michael Dukakis over Bush's dad in the last election.

Schieffer says Bush quickly let him know that they weren't putting together a Republican group or a Democratic group; they were putting together an ownership group, and politics didn't matter. Thus began Schieffer's saga with the Rangers: From his start as a minority investor with the Bush group, he would go on to become the visionary behind the building of The Ballpark and a significant figure in Rangers history.

In the end, the Bush group had 16 investors. On March 18, 1989, they purchased the Texas Rangers from Fort Worth oilman Eddie Chiles for $86 million.

None of the individual investors would have more than a 12 percent share. Bush's share, in fact, was paltry: He had borrowed $500,000 for his initial investment; he would later add another $106,000, for a total ownership share of about 1.8 percent. His fellow owners would later gift him with another 10 percent for putting the deal together. When the team was sold to Tom Hicks for $250 million in June of 1998, Bush would walk away with almost $15 million. Not a bad return on a $600,000 investment.

$$\sim \quad \sim \quad \sim$$

WITH THE SALE to the Bush group a done deal in April 1989, for the first time in their history, the Rangers had "professional" ownership, with structure, organization and a plan moving forward. The ownership group was divided into committees, according to their various areas of expertise. Schieffer, a true baseball fan with a deep love for the game and its history, was named "ballpark czar" and entrusted with the most important assignment of all: to build a new ballpark.

First, though, they had to figure out where to build it. It was never a foregone conclusion that the Rangers would stay in Arlington, and the need for a new ballpark gave the new ownership group leverage to make a financially friendly deal.

"We told [the city of] Arlington that, if you can put a deal together that will work for us, we're ready to stay," Schieffer said. But Arlington was competing against four other Metroplex cities — Irving, Plano, Dallas and Frisco — that had expressed interest. "I met with the mayors of all five cities," Schieffer said. The last was Arlington Mayor Richard Greene.

"He said, 'I don't see how you could have a better location. The problem in Phoenix or LA or DFW is that they are all horizontal cities. They're spread out. You have to be able to draw people from all over,'" Schieffer recalled.

At that meeting in his office in City Hall, Greene recalls, "I surrounded him with stacks of research that we had done that covered everything from how to finance a new ballpark, via Wall Street bonds secured by a new sales tax; engineering and architecture studies; even a working model of what we projected as a new ballpark and my certainty we would have the public support needed to deliver on our vision.

"Among the exhibits was a giant map mounted on a foldable foam-core board. Tom began to study that more than anything else and asked if he could take it with him when he left my office. I had no idea what kind of car he had but told him, absolutely, we'll get in his vehicle somehow."

At home, Schieffer spread out the map of the 147 acres where Arlington Stadium sat and took a paperweight from his desk to stand in for a new ballpark.

"I started moving it around," Schieffer recalls, "putting it in various places where a new park could be located. The key was the 147 acres of real estate; that was the hidden value."

The north side of the property, bounded by Copeland Road and Interstate 30, already had built-in value. Placing the ballpark nearer the back of the property would naturally create value for that area of land. But to make Schieffer's strategic plan work, they needed still more space — more property.

A developer named Moises Mondelac owned 60 acres of land south of Randol Mill Road he'd purchased for $6.50 a square foot. It was debt-free, and the economic downturn had Mondelac looking for a buyer. The timing was right.

Mike Reilly, a minority member of the Rangers group and a local

Carolyn Bauman, Courtesy, Fort Worth Star-Telegram Collection, Special Collections, The University of Texas at Arlington Libraries

George W. Bush, left, announced Tom Schieffer as the Rangers' new team president during a 1991 press conference at Arlington Stadium.

real estate developer, took a blind option to buy the land for $2.67 a square foot. The blind option meant Mondelac didn't know who the new owners would be, and that's the way Bush and company wanted it: If Mondelac guessed that the new Rangers owners were the ones who were interested, he might jack up the price.

Schieffer picks up the story: "We go to the closing, and the lawyer representing Moises, Parker Nelson, says, 'Wait a minute. Mike Reilly there went to high school with Tom Schieffer. This could be the Rangers buying this land.' Moises said, 'I don't care, I just want the money.' So the deal closes. We knew then with the existing acreage we could build a ballpark."

Schieffer's next two calls were to Greene and Vandergriff.

"I said, 'If y'all are prepared to do a deal, and if you both can come to my office tomorrow, we can see if we can make a deal.

"There were 18 deal points — what we would do, what the Rangers would do, what the city would do, what the county would do. In an hour we had agreed on 17 deal points. I left the two of them in my office for an hour. Then they opened the door and said, 'We have a deal.'"

The 18th point?

"I don't even remember what it was," Schieffer said. "It really wasn't significant."

In the end, Schieffer said, negotiating the deal "wasn't hard, because we did it as a partnership; it's not like someone was trying to take advantage of the other."

Greene agrees: "The Rangers' new owners could have *both* a new ballpark *and* the potential of real estate development — virtually unlimited opportunity."

And less than three months later, in January 1991, voters by a 2-to-1 margin approved a new bond bill to make the project happen.

Greene credits Arlington voters "with saving the Rangers and preserving the Vandergriff legacy that would otherwise have drifted into history."

He believes that "literally everything that has happened in the city's largest economy — in the entertainment district — can be traced to that 1991 election victory.

"Without it, Jerry Jones would not have noticed Arlington [as a prospective home for the Dallas Cowboys]. He told me that when he said he had studied the ballpark deal and how Arlington achieved the outcome," Greene recalls.

"Without that victory, maybe Arlington Stadium would have found some kind of continued use, but likely it would be demolished, and the only thing left out there [would be] some roller coasters in the Six Flags park."

Chapter 12

THE TEMPLE
Tom Schieffer's Dream

*A*T THE END *of the 1990s, the Rangers were on the threshold of a new era. The deal that had been struck between the new owners, fronted by George W. Bush, and the city of Arlington had kept the Rangers in Arlington. Getting a deal done was one thing, though — building a new ballpark was another. Luckily, the Bush group had a secret weapon: Tom Schieffer.*

IT WAS SO BEAUTIFUL, so pure and true to the spirit of the game, it could make you weep.

So awe-inspiring was The Ballpark in Arlington that the first time my colleague Randy Galloway walked through the portal behind home plate and gazed upon its sweeping grandeur, he was reduced to one word, which he repeated over and over again as he gazed about . . .

"*Mother-----r!*"

Exactly.

Claire Smith, the Baseball Hall of Fame columnist for the *New York Times*, was stunned by the beauty and grace of The Ballpark in Arlington. Here's some of what she wrote:

That this park stands out so, with its outer walls topped by a crown of arches, is no mistake. Even though the American League team insisted that its brand-new facility be a traditional "people's place," a cozy park as opposed to a cold, impersonal stadium, it's still big-hearted enough to make it quintessentially Texan.

Filled with bravura and sun-filled bleachers that wrap around the foul poles and reach high into the sky, The Ballpark in Arlington, ap-

proximately 1,400,000 square feet, radiates the vastness of the plains that surround it.

If you had grown up rooting for the Rangers during their tough years in Arlington Stadium, walking into The Ballpark made you feel you'd died and gone to baseball heaven. This wasn't just a ballpark, it was a shrine. Just listen to the recollections of Dallas sports radio legend Mike Rhyner:

"If you will recall, as the place was going up, they had media availability to see the place during various stages of construction, and the media could go in and look around," Rhyner said. "I never did that, even though I wanted to. I wanted my first look at it to be with real baseball." On April 1, 1994, Rhyner and his "Hardline" show crew headed to The Ballpark for its debut, an exhibition game against the New York Mets. Rhyner had read what others had to say about the new stadium. He'd heard the praise and the accolades. But the gravelly voiced talk-show host, famous for his prickly independent streak, would judge for himself.

"I was not expecting the reality of it," said Rhyner.

Reporting his first impressions on the air, he noted:

"That's no ballpark; that transcends the concept of ballpark ... that's a temple."

From that point on, to Rhyner and his listeners, that's what it would always be: "The Temple."

~ ~ ~

WHEN THE IDEA of his becoming the "ballpark czar" was first broached within the new Rangers ownership group, Schieffer recalls, "I went home to [his wife] Suzanne and said, "You'll never guess what George and Rusty asked me to do — build a ballpark — but I turned them down.

"Then Suzanne said, 'You might only have a chance to build a ballpark once in your life.'"

The next day, Schieffer went back to Bush and Rose and accepted the biggest challenge of his life.

Yes, he would build a ballpark, and it would be like no other, because ballparks, Schieffer believed, are like a family's home. This would be the Rangers' custom-built *home.*

"When you walk into a warehouse, no one remembers what it looks like; there are no distinguishing features," Schieffer said. "It's just one big room. But in a home, there are places that people identify with and grow comfortable being. We tried to create those spaces for our fans. There was no area that had more than 2,700 seats in it that were the same."

Contrast that to Arlington Stadium, where 17,000 of its 43,521 seats were identical $4 bleacher seats.

"We wanted to build a *ballpark*," Schieffer said. "I think a ballpark is different than the field any other sport plays in, because each is unique. What we were trying to do was create something that would be unique and would recognize the history of the game.

"We were trying to figure out why people loved ballparks, as opposed to stadiums and arenas. As I toured the classic ballparks around baseball, I realized that they had each had distinctive features, especially in the outfield. We thought it was important to create small areas that people would eventually identify with."

"Fan-friendly" wasn't just a throwaway line for Schieffer. He wanted to build a ballpark that would be spacious and comfortable, yet with an intimacy that would make the fans feel like they were part of the game.

"We elevated the bullpens so that the fans could sit out there and watch the relievers warm up," Schieffer said. "I had four seats out there myself. You felt like you were in the game, you were so close to those guys warming up. The players would come up and talk. Those were just bleachers, but they were great seats."

The visitors' bullpen, on the other hand, required a different strategy, one that Schieffer hoped would give the home team an edge. The idea came from Rangers pitcher Kenny Rogers, who would later author the only perfect game ever thrown at The Ballpark in Arlington.

"Kenny told me you don't want the opposing reliever to be comfortable. So we had them warming up facing the opposite direction they would be pitching in the game. We made sure there were no square corners in that bullpen."

When the Rangers' pitching coach, Dick Bosman, toured the park for the first time, he told Schieffer, "I love the park, but you guys really made a lot of mistakes in that visitors' bullpen. It's all jumbled up."

Perfect, Schieffer said.

If you're wondering why Bush and Co. didn't just go ahead and build a domed stadium, there were a couple of reasons. One was that it was cost-prohibitive at the time. The development of retractable roofs was still in its infant stages. None of the communities interested in the team had the money for an air-conditioned domed stadium, nor did the Rangers' ownership.

Second, and perhaps most importantly:

"George and I believe that baseball should be played outdoors," Schieffer said.

Nothing was going to change the effects of a Texas summer: It would be hot, but the Rangers would do what they could. Wind studies were done and experts brought in to do temperature evaluations in various parts of the park at certain times of the day. They would use Major League Baseball's waiver to play night games, even on getaway days (that would change in the early 2000s under manager Buck Showalter) and Sundays. Wind screens were erected to help direct a breeze toward the seating bowl.

(Some of that technology would be negated in later years: After the Bush ownership sold the franchise in June of 1988, new owner Tom Hicks would subsequently build a stadium club behind home plate, effectively plugging a major air-flow area. A new electronic ribbon advertising board added just below the lower suites also created more heat in the bowl seating area.)

Schieffer brought in Washington architect David Schwartz to execute his vision of what a Texas ballpark should be. It would include rustic red-brick and pink-granite walls, towers at all four corners and a four-story outfield office building at center field. There was even a "secret" apartment, accessible through the Rangers' offices on the fourth floor, where owners or others in for a visit might spend the night. I did that myself one night after a game and wrote a column about the hideaway.

Schieffer didn't want a cookie-cutter ballpark. He didn't want a multi-purpose stadium. He wanted something unique, something Texan, something the Rangers franchise and its fans could be proud of. He put his heart and soul into building a monument to the great game of baseball.

And the new stadium would change the fortunes of the franchise in ways that no one could have imagined.

"It was a pretty sad-sack franchise when we bought it," Schieffer said. "It was always just kind of trying to keep the doors open. The ballpark changed everything. When we bought the team, the revenues were something under $30 million. The last year at Arlington Stadium, I think we had $60 million in revenues. The first year of the new ballpark, we had $127 million."

~ ~ ~

THE BALLPARK would eventually be superseded by a new facility, Globe Life Field, a multipurpose venue that would become the Rangers' new home in 2020.

Today's Globe Life Field, with its retractable roof, its air-conditioning and its adjacent hotel-dining-entertainment-retail-events complex, is undeniably a comfortable place to watch sporting events. But it lacks many of the elements that made The Ballpark such a special place: the classic design, the sweeping grandeur, the aura of nostalgia.

Even when The Ballpark was brand-new, there was always a sense in its red-brick walls of baseball history lurking right around the corner. Entering the new multi-purpose facility, with its utilitarian feel, brings no emotional tug at the heart — certainly nothing like the feeling that was evoked by walking through that home-plate portal and emerging into the great bowl of The Ballpark, with the brilliant sunshine glistening off the emerald natural grass; the deep umber of the infield dirt; the spectacular, soaring Home Run Porch.

The Ballpark was a place where Joe DiMaggio or Willie Mays or Mickey Mantle would have been comfortable roaming center field, where they would have felt perfectly at home.

Schieffer, who grew up rooting for the Fort Worth Cats at La Grave Field, remembers a vignette from opening day at The Ballpark in Arlington in 1994. He and general manager Tom Grieve are sitting on the bench in the Rangers' first-base dugout a couple of hours before game time. Grieve, who was an outfielder with the team in Washington before it moved to Texas, is shaking his head as he stares out at the field.

"He kept saying, 'I can't believe this is our ballpark,'" Schieffer said. "Over and over ... 'I can't believe this is our ballpark.'"

Grieve, who in 2022 was in his 28th season as the team's color TV analyst, remembers that moment, too.

"After the years of getting here, playing in the old ballpark ... I loved that old ballpark; the fans loved coming to it; it's the first place I played here," Grieve said. "I have nothing but fond memories of that [original] ballpark. I don't know that I ever envisioned [the Rangers] playing anywhere else but that ballpark.

"But I'm looking out at The Ballpark in Arlington, taking in how beautiful it was, and it was just a moment when it dawned on me: *I can't believe this is ours ... I can't believe this is ours ...* it was overwhelming."

It was never just the bricks and mortar, or the convenience of more restrooms and concession options. It wasn't even entirely about the increased revenue the ballpark would produce through its two levels of luxury suites, or its private clubs. After two-plus decades of getting by in a converted minor-league stadium with almost no defining features or ambience, what Schieffer had accomplished was as much about a feeling as it was about physical change, though there was obviously plenty of that.

Grieve's reaction was universal. Now there was pride, a sense of finally belonging, a growing confidence, a belief that anything might be possible ... even a World Series. This newfound conviction was felt everywhere, from the players to the front office staff to the fans, even to the media.

Columnist Mac Engel summed it up in the *Fort Worth Star-Telegram* in late March of 2020, as the Rangers were preparing to play their final season in Schieffer's Dream before the move to the new Globe Life Park.

"Whatever your thoughts are on the new park, the legacy of 'the old place' [The Ballpark in Arlington] is that there are no Texas Rangers without Schieffer's efforts to design and build The Ballpark in Arlington. Without the Ballpark, the Rangers are the Oakland A's ... if they are lucky."

Dallas Morning News sports columnist Kevin Sherrington chimed in with his observations near the end of that season:

"No matter what your opinion on the need for an air-conditioned stadium, the job Schieffer did with the place across the street made the Rangers a big-league club. The decisions he made not only determined where it sat and looked, but how it played. He formed an identity for a franchise that had been lost in the weeds. The cash flow from the facility that opened in 1994 enabled the Rangers to compete with the big boys, leading to the organization's first playoff appearances and two World Series. Basically, most of the franchise's best memories."

This is not meant to disparage the Rangers' new stadium, Globe Life Field. I don't even mind the exterior that so many have ridiculed. Call it the Shed or the Hangar or whatever, its cutting-edge technology is obvious. It's a comfortable — and expensive — place to sit. Current Rangers ownership believes it can make more money in the new stadium. That's the bottom line.

But it was The Ballpark in Arlington that put the Texas Rangers on the map in Major League Baseball. No longer would they be the trailer-trash relative relegated to the wrong side of the tracks.

It was where Juan Gonzalez and Raffy Palmeiro boomed home runs, where Pudge Rodriguez became a Hall of Famer, where Neftali Feliz once struck out Alex Rodriguez to send the Rangers to the World Series.

"When we cut the ribbon on the ballpark, it changed everything," said Schieffer. "It allowed us to be a major-league team. I don't say it in a mean sort of way, but [before The Ballpark] it was a major league-franchise in name but not in reality. We made it a major-league franchise, and we were proud of that."

~ ~ ~

FOR THOSE who were involved in this new era for the Rangers, lives were changed, too: Tom Schieffer, who became ambassador to Australia and later Japan; George W. Bush, who showed he could successfully run a major-league team and, eventually, the country; even the reluctant co-partner Rusty Rose, who came out of his shell to give the occasional interview or observation to those of us he came to know.

Rose, in fact, "became almost obsessive" about baseball, Schieffer said. "He wanted the franchise to be something people would be proud of."

As for George W. Bush, a cynic — and there are lots of us lurking in the weeds — might believe that becoming involved with the Rangers was simply a calculated strategy to polish his resume in hopes of resurrecting his political career, perhaps for a governorship or a senatorial bid.

Tom Schieffer, a man with some personal experience in politics, is not one of those people.

"It was not a political opportunity to him," insisted Schieffer. "It was the opportunity to own a baseball team. Anyone trying to build a narrative that says George's ownership in the team was purely a political strategy is simply wrong."

If Bush's motivation *was* political, though, he certainly pulled it off like a grand chess master. The same year that The Ballpark in Arlington opened in 1994, Bush was elected governor of Texas with a surprising upset of popular Democratic incumbent Ann Richards. Seven years later, in 2001, he was elected president.

"I frankly think [owning the Rangers] changed George's life in the sense that it gave him an identity apart from his father," said Schieffer.

"He was the guy who ran the Rangers, and he was good at it. He was good with the fans, and he kept the partnership together. The three of us never had a disagreement. As a result, that also permeated the organization. There was leadership in the franchise that had not been there before."

In many ways, Bush did become the face of the Rangers. Rare was the night when he wasn't parked in his seat alongside the home dugout, boots propped up on the rail, munching peanuts, chatting amiably with whatever Rangers hitter might be on deck. One night it might be Nolan Ryan and wife Ruth joining George and Laura. The next it might be his dad, former president George Walker Bush, and his mom Barbara.

George W. could have reclined in air-conditioned comfort in a private suite whenever he wanted. Instead, he took his place among the fans, comfortable, easygoing, approachable. He was just what the doctor ordered as the outgoing, personable owner of the Rangers.

Even better, he had a magnificent stadium in which to hold court.

IT HAD been a given that whoever bought the Rangers from Eddie Chiles would eventually require a new stadium to make the team a profitable enterprise.

But only the Bush group had Tom Schieffer, a man with a vision. And it is fair to say that only Tom Schieffer could have built The Ballpark in Arlington.

Those of us who came to love The Ballpark in Arlington can fairly make the case that Schieffer built the most beautiful baseball facility ever, a monument that reflected both his Texas heritage and his love and respect for the game's history. It would change the face of the Texas Rangers franchise forever.

To us, as radio's Mike Rhyner so vividly and reverently proclaimed, The Ballpark in Arlington was and always will be "The Temple."

Chapter 13

THE CRUCIBLE
The Faith of Johnny Oates

*A FTER YEARS OF FAILURE, of teases, of almosts, the Texas Rang-
ers were on the verge of finally breaking through with an American League West championship in 1996, holding a nine-game lead in
September.*

*Then, suddenly, they quit winning. They lost, and lost, and lost
again. They stared into the abyss of failure when triumph was so close.
It was a trial by fire that would test even the faith of devout manager
Johnny Oates.*

JOHNNY OATES SITS ALONE at his desk in the visiting manager's
office in Seattle's Kingdome. When I peek in, his head is bowed, supported by his right hand, his elbow resting on the desk. I'm not sure if
he's praying or weeping. Whichever it is, I don't interrupt.

Pray hard, I think. Pray very, very hard.

~ ~ ~

IT WAS Sept. 19, 1996, and the Texas Rangers were embroiled in
their first real American League West Division pennant race. After
being in first place for all but three days since the season began, they
had just seen a nine-game lead over the Mariners shrink to two in a
mere nine days. They were crawling out of Seattle after being swept in
a key four-game series. They had lost eight of their last nine. Frankly,
they smelled like roadkill. I know. I watched their agony every step
of the way.

It was definitely time to pray.

Or perhaps to scream, which is what Oates had been doing moments before the doors of the visiting clubhouse were opened to the media after the Rangers' 7-6 loss in the series finale in Seattle.

Oates wasn't normally a screamer. He much preferred a calm, measured, professional approach. This situation, though, called for something a little more drastic.

In desperation, Oates pulled one of the oldest managerial tricks in the book: reaming out his team in an epic rant. To punctuate the tirade, he flipped over the post-game food table — and threw his back out.

Being Johnny, he continued his harangue without missing a beat, but the players could see the anguish in his expression.

"We were all worried about whether he was OK, but we couldn't show it," recalled Mark McLemore, who was playing second base for the Rangers at the time and is now one of the Rangers' pre-and-post-game TV analysts. "We knew he did it, but he kept going like he wasn't hurting. He continued to light us up for a little bit after that.

"Johnny was calm and cool most of the time, but he could go to the other side with the best of them, in a heartbeat. Fortunately, we didn't give him reason very often."

The 1996 Rangers were a veteran-laden team. McLemore, first baseman Will Clark, shortstop Kevin Elster, center fielder Darryl Hamilton, designated hitter Mickey Tettleton, along with pitchers John Burkett and Ken Hill, had all been around the block a few times.

"None of the players were in a panic," McLemore recalled. "We were veteran guys. People, the media, were talking about past history, but that had nothing to do with us. We just had to take care of now.

"Everybody talks about different guys being leaders on that team, but we had a bunch of veteran players. Everybody knew what they needed to do. The young guys, like Rusty [Greer] and Darren [Oliver] just followed suit.

"If you needed extra work, if you needed to back off a little bit, you just went out and did it. There wasn't a day we didn't go out there ready to win. We may not have always done it, but we were ready."

OK, Mac, if you say so. But what it looked like to most of the baseball world was that the Rangers were choking on their own sordid history of catastrophe. That's what it felt like to those of us who were documenting that suffocating 10-day spiral into Dante's Inferno. The tension was so thick around the team, the atmosphere so heavy, that drawing a deep breath was almost impossible.

"We're not just fighting the Mariners, or the A's, or the Angels," a desperate Oates confided at one point during the collapse. "We're fighting ghosts. We're fighting more than three decades of failure here. It's like we're trying to carry an anvil to the finish line."

It wasn't like Oates to show cracks in his armor. He made a point of stoicism. Weakness was not something he entertained. He was also a man of faith, a dedicated and committed Christian.

No one had to ask where Johnny Oates stood when it came to God. He would tell you in a heartbeat. At the same time, I was making slow but methodical progress on my own Christian walk. There were many times when Johnny walked beside me on that journey. A few years later, when he was diagnosed with terminal brain cancer, it would be my turn to walk with him.

The Rangers had finished second in the AL West on five occasions (1974, 1977, 1978, 1981, 1986). Not one of those seasons could be called a real pennant race. The closest the Rangers finished to the eventual winner in any of those years was five games; they had not been a serious threat in any of them.

The one time they might have had a legitimate shot at the playoffs had come two years earlier, in the aborted 1994 season. The Rangers were leading the West by a half-game when baseball went off the rails on Aug. 11. The players, who had been working under the old collective-bargaining agreement while negotiating a new deal with the owners, gave up on the negotiations at that point and walked off the job. The owners canceled the playoffs and the World Series that year.

Now, two years later, the Rangers were experiencing the crucible of a pennant race for the first time, hoping to close the deal at last.

~ ~ ~

A SIMPLE split of their mid-September four-game series in Seattle would have all but sewn up their first division title in the Rangers' 25th year since arriving in Texas. But the charging Mariners, in the midst of a 10-game win streak, were threatening to duplicate their comeback of a year earlier, when they'd run down the Angels in the stretch to capture their first West Division crown.

As I pored through the *Fort Worth Star-Telegram* archives researching this book, I encountered something that made me wonder if I might have been at least partially responsible for the curse that had suddenly descended on the Rangers in the second week of September of 1996.

It was there in black and white on Page 1 of the sports section on Sept 12, 1996, dateline Toronto. The headline on my column that day:

Don't laugh, but Rangers could win it all

As I was writing that opinion piece, feverishly making a case that the Rangers were capable of not just finally making the playoffs but actually winning a pennant and the World Series, they were in the process of having a five-game winning streak snapped by the Blue Jays in the finale of a three-game set at the Skydome.

I blame Jays manager Cito Gaston for my overexuberance.

"I think they have a chance to win it all," he'd told me before the game. "I think they could go all the way."

Oh, Canada! I felt like Uma Thurman in the "Pulp Fiction" scene where she gets the adrenaline shot straight to the heart.

Three years earlier, the Blue Jays had upset Philadelphia for their first World Series championship. I figured Cito, of all people, must know when a team has what it takes. He pointed out how well the Rangers had played against the heavyweights in the AL East and against Central Division leader Cleveland, too.

"They've played some of the best teams in the league and played them well," Gaston said. "I think they have an excellent chance of riding that momentum all the way through the postseason."

Cito was telling me exactly what I wanted to hear — what any Rangers fan wanted to hear. The column was practically writing itself. It didn't occur to me that there could be a huge personal reason Cito believed the Rangers might be world-beaters: He was looking at it from the perspective of a manager who had watched his team lose 10 out of 12 to the Texans that season, being outscored 72-45 in the process.

At that point in the season, the Rangers had still held a more-than-comfortable nine-game lead over Seattle with just 17 to play. There was no hint that an 8-3 loss to the Jays that Thursday afternoon would trigger the most stressful stretch of games in Rangers history. One small storm cloud loomed on the horizon: The Rangers still had to visit Seattle's depressing Kingdome for four games.

Some stadiums just seem cursed for some teams. Back in the

Texas Rangers

Under manager Johnny Oates, the Rangers were 1998 AL West champs but were defeated by the New York Yankees in the AL Division Series.

early 1980s, for example, former Rangers manager Doug Rader had dubbed Toronto's Exhibition Stadium — the Blue Jays' home before the Skydome was built — the "Voodoo Palace" because of the strange ways his team lost games there. He hated the place with a passion.

By the mid-'90s, as far as the Rangers were concerned, Seattle's Kingdome had become the "Doo-Doo Palace." Going into that fateful four-game series, the Rangers had lost 16 of their last 19 games there. It was about to get even worse.

"Everybody feared going into that place," Doug Melvin recalled from his home in Park City, Utah. As the Rangers' general manager from 1995 to 2001, Melvin had a front-row seat for the disaster that was about to unfold in the Kingdome. "The lighting was bad; you had to worry about [hitting] the roof. There was definitely a home-field advantage there."

In Game 1, the Mariners started changeup artist Jamie Moyer. Moyer had been released by the Rangers in 1990, a move Bobby Valentine was later to call his biggest mistake as a manager. The left-hander didn't throw hard enough to rend a wet Kleenex, but he stifled the Rangers on four hits, and Seattle easily won 6-0. It was not a good omen for the visitors.

The next night Terry Mulholland, another left-hander, retired the first 15 Rangers in order, and shortstop Kevin Elster's error keyed a four-run sixth inning for Seattle. The Mariners won, 5-2. The avalanche was picking up speed.

"I remember the feeling of inevitability at the Kingdome each night, that we were going to lose," said Rangers radio broadcaster Eric Nadel. "I remember the level of anxiety I felt each night at batting practice.

"Johnny [Oates] was trying to hide it, but he definitely was not calm. He was whistling a lot, and humming a lot, which he would do when he was nervous."

In Game 3, Texas slugger Juan González belted his 45th homer, a two-run shot to left, off Seattle starter Sterling Hitchcock in the fourth. But then Rangers starter Bobby Witt served up a three-run blast to the Mariners' Jay Buhner, erasing the two-run Texas lead. The Rangers, gasping for air in an increasingly claustrophobic Kingdome, meekly surrendered after that, going hitless over the final five innings.

On the Mariners' sound system, someone cued the theme from "Jaws." There was blood in the water, and the sharks were circling.

The next morning, a shell-shocked Doug Melvin, his special assistant Sandy Johnson, club president Tom Schieffer and TV color analyst Tom Grieve drove out to Snoqualmie Falls for brunch at the famed Salish Lodge in the Cascade Mountains east of Seattle. Schieffer, Melvin and Johnson had traveled to Seattle because they were convinced the Rangers might clinch the division on the trip. Instead, they found themselves living a nightmare.

As the four men gazed out over the beautiful falls, thundering some 270 feet to the rocks below, Melvin turned to his companions and joked, "Don't let me jump."

The smiles and half-hearted chuckles didn't last long. Neither did Rangers starter Roger Pavlik that night, surviving just two innings as the Mariners won 7-6 to complete the sweep.

The loss chopped the Texas lead to a shaky two games. Then Oates demolished the post-game food table, pulling a muscle in his back, and the Rangers boarded their flight to Anaheim, where rock bottom still awaited their unabated plunge.

It would come only 24 hours later, as the Rangers and Angels kicked off a three-game series at the Big A.

~ ~ ~

WITH THE SCORE tied 4-4 after nine innings in the first game of the three-game set, Mark McLemore singled home Dean Palmer in the top of the 10th to give the Rangers a 5-4 lead. Just three measly outs and the skid would finally end. The sighs of relief from the Rangers' contingent were a bit premature, however.

In the bottom of the inning, with nobody on and the Rangers just one out away from finally ending their rapid descent into Hades, Angels pinch-hitter George Arias and second baseman Rex Hudler each lined two-out singles off Texas reliever Mike Stanton.

Oates could have summoned closer Mike Henneman to face the Angels' left-handed hitter Garret Anderson, but Henneman had been struggling of late. With the lefty-on-lefty advantage, Oates elected to stick with Stanton, who had been pitching well since being obtained from Boston at the July 31 trade deadline. California's veteran outfielder foiled the strategy by slamming Stanton's 1-2 fastball into left center for a two-run walk-off double.

The Angels had won, 6-5, handing the Rangers their fifth straight loss, the eighth in their last nine games. In Seattle, meanwhile, the Mariners paddled Oakland 12-2 for their ninth consecutive victory. The Rangers' lead was down to a single game. They had finally escaped the hated Kingdome only to have their hearts ripped out in the shadow of the Magic Kingdom.

"After that game, Tom Schieffer, Sandy Johnson and I walked back to the hotel, and not one word was said," Melvin recalled. "I guess whenever you walk back to the hotel and your boss is with you and you don't say anything, there is a bit of nervousness."

That game was the low point, McLemore said. "Guys were starting to get pissed off. We knew we needed to play better than this and we needed to play better than this right now. We knew we weren't playing to our capabilities."

In the clubhouse, the atmosphere was grim. For the first time, there were grumblings about pitch selection, managerial decisions, misplays. Players were pointing fingers at each other, playing the blame game. Catcher Pudge Rodríguez was targeted by some of his teammates for calling for a fastball from Stanton after the left-hander had made Anderson look bad with his slider. It was a petty critique, but after 10 days of frustration, the sniping was not surprising.

"It's human nature," Oates told me at the time. "I do it. I try to keep it private, between Boz [pitching coach Dick Bosman] and me, but I still do it sometimes."

Natural or not, it was a bad look. Pettiness always is. The negative vibes were threatening to spill out of control.

"Some of those guys may have been worn down," Rangers executive vice president for communications John Blake pointed out later. "Johnny played a set lineup every day. The bench never played. There had to be a little bit of fatigue after playing almost every day in Texas."

There was also no escaping Rangers history. They had been in first place at the All-Star break on several occasions. They had always faded. They had to prove they could climb the mountain before anyone would believe they could actually do it.

"If you'd been around here a long time, been through Rangers collapses, it was always like, 'The Rangers are going to fade,'" said Blake, who vividly remembers that particular series-opening loss in Anaheim and what a gut punch it was.

"A lot of us were thinking, if we blow a nine-game lead, will we ever recover from it as a franchise?" Blake said. "If we hadn't won, if we'd collapsed completely, what might have changed?"

It was Oates who redirected the narrative — and probably saved the Rangers' season.

He came to the ballpark the next day somehow as relaxed as I'd ever seen him. No nervous humming. No scowls or snippy answers to questions. He was smiling, completely at ease. Looking at him, talking to him, you'd have thought the Rangers had won 10 in a row instead of dropping eight of their last nine games.

The change in his demeanor was noticeable to everyone around him that day.

"I remember how composed Johnny was," Blake said. "I remember before we opened the clubhouse to the media the next day after the extra-inning loss, Johnny just had this air of confidence. Johnny could get moody, but I remember that day him having this aura of 'We got this.'"

Oates' positive vibes seemed to envelop the whole team. The tension that had been so suffocating began to lift, like humidity after a fresh cool front.

"I remember feeling really good about the fact that [John] Burkett was pitching that night," broadcaster Nadel said.

Like Stanton, Burkett was a key piece in the Texas rotation that

Melvin had acquired for the stretch run in a trade with the Florida Marlins in the first week of August. The Rangers had given up Ryan Dempster and a player-to-be-named-later (Rick Helling) for the veteran right-hander. Burkett had shut out the Blue Jays for a huge win in Toronto. But nothing would be bigger than the win at Anaheim on Saturday, Sept. 21.

Handed a 3-0 lead in the third, including solo home runs by Rusty Greer, fresh off the disabled list, and Juan González, Burkett was in complete control. He would give up just a single run in eight innings as the Rangers rolled, 7-1.

In the visiting clubhouse after the game, it was as if the sun had broken through a thick layer of dark clouds after days and days of storms. It didn't even matter that the Mariners had hammered Oakland 9-2 in the Kingdome and that the Rangers' lead in the West was still just one slim game. Suddenly, the Rangers' confidence was back.

"It changed everything," Nadel said. "When they lost that Friday game, blowing the division title seemed inevitable. After Burkett won that game [Saturday], I felt totally differently. Then when they won the next day, too, behind [Ken] Hill, I figured things would be OK."

What Burkett started Hill finished, tossing a complete-game 7-1 win on Sunday afternoon to nudge Texas' lead back to a sinus-clearing two games when Seattle lost at home to the A's, 13-11. That loss finally snapped the Mariners' 10-game win streak. It was also the first time in 11 days that the Mariners had lost on the same day that the Rangers won.

The Rangers would split the final two games of the road trip in Oakland. With Seattle suddenly losing three in a row, the Rangers flew back to Texas with a three-game lead and just four to play against the struggling Angels.

Ironically, there would be no glorious victory to kick off the Rangers' first division championship celebration. Instead, it would sneak in quietly and awkwardly while they were mired in a 15-inning marathon that they would eventually lose 4-3 to the Angels in the wee hours of the morning at Arlington Stadium.

At 11:52 p.m., as the Rangers and Angels struggled fitfully onward, the news flashed on the scoreboard at The Ballpark in Arlington: Oakland 8, Seattle 1. The Rangers were champions at last.

The team's celebration, however, would have to wait until their own game was finished. Finally, in the top of the 15th, California pushed across a couple of runs. The Rangers could counter with only one in the bottom of the frame.

As a small group of diehard fans clustered behind the home dugout, chanting and cheering, the exhausted Rangers filed into their plastic-sheet-lined clubhouse. They lit up victory cigars and sprayed each other with beer and champagne in the traditional championship celebration they had waited a quarter of a century to enjoy.

THE RANGERS would go on to win the first game of the best-of-five series in Yankee Stadium, 6-2, then to lose the next three, despite five home runs and nine RBIs from Juan González, who earned the nickname "Señor Octobre," the Hispanic equivalent of Hall of Famer Reggie Jackson's "Mr. October." Gonzalez would be named American League most valuable player. Oates, who kept the faith, was named the league's manager of the year.

But the mystery remains: What happened between Friday night's devastating extra-inning loss to the Angels and that Saturday afternoon when Oates got to the Big A wearing an incredibly confident smile? What suddenly gave Oates the peace of mind to arrive at the ballpark with such an aura of tranquility and calm that it would infect the whole team?

Yeah, it's a "softball" question. His strong Christian faith was an integral part of who Johnny Oates was after he came to Texas. At the end of his first spring as Rangers manager, in 1995, Oates had received an emergency phone call from his daughter Lori. His wife Gloria was in the middle of a psychological crisis, brought on by the stress of raising a family while her husband was constantly absent. She was shutting down, telling Johnny on the phone that she was ready to die.

"Baseball doesn't even stop for death," she told him.

The thought of losing Gloria, his wife of almost 30 years at the time, frightened Oates as nothing ever had before. He asked the Rangers for a leave of absence and rushed to his wife's side. He would miss the first five games of his initial season as Rangers manager.

The crisis changed Oates. He was already a Christian, but together he and Gloria rededicated themselves to their faith. It was where they both sought answers and found solace and comfort.

The thing that gave Oates such serenity that day in Anaheim was time spent talking to God. Johnny told me so himself, and his wife Gloria confirmed it too.

"I can remember Mark McLemore telling me that Johnny came to the ballpark whistling, and that all the players were amazed at his attitude," Gloria Oates told me. "I'm sure he had confirmation from the Lord to just keep taking one step at a time."

It was the same peace, the same faith, that Oates carried with him after he was diagnosed with an aggressive malignant brain tumor in November of 2001. A month later, I flew to Richmond, rented a car and drove to their home in Matoaca, Va., to spend time with Johnny and Gloria. Johnny had just undergone surgery to remove part of the tumor. The average lifespan following the surgery, doctors said, was 14 to 18 months. Oates had other plans.

It was mid-December when I drove Johnny to Richmond for one of his radiation treatments. We talked about life, and death, and faith, and that terrible nine-day stretch in 1996 when the world seemed to be crashing down around his ears.

What, I asked him, had gotten him through that crisis? How could he show up at the ballpark in Anaheim with a smile and a whistle that day, after the Rangers' lead in the West had been slashed to a single game, when before he had been visibly seething with turmoil?

Simple, he said softly. He had spent time talking with God.

"I didn't pray to win," he told me. "I prayed for His will to be done. And I realized, at some point, that I could live with that."

It was almost Christmas, and Oates had been released from the hospital after his surgery only a couple of weeks earlier. The three Oates children had set up the family Christmas tree as a special "welcome home" gift for their dad. There were no presents piled under the impressively decorated tree. Instead, Gloria had arranged photos of the real gifts in their lives — their children, grandchildren, family. It was a poignant gesture of love and appreciation of what was most important in their lives.

"I wanted to celebrate life," Gloria said, "and to celebrate the life that was given to us and for us."

It was particularly appropriate for someone like Johnny, whose disdain for the relentless commercialization of Christmas had made it nearly impossible for him to enjoy the season over the years. Always a worrier, he fretted about those who would have little or nothing to celebrate.

This one would not be Johnny's last Christmas, despite the doctors' timeline. He would see the holiday pass again in 2002 and then in 2003. In December of 2004, though, Oates found himself growing weaker every day. As the days ticked by toward Christmas, Gloria was astonished to hear her husband say he was really looking forward to the holiday. His change in attitude left her confused.

Then it dawned on her. Johnny was looking forward to Christmas because he'd be spending it with Jesus. She knew it would have been just like the meticulous Oates to make such an arrangement.

He died early that Christmas Eve morning.

WHAT I KNOW for sure is that, when the Rangers arrived in Anaheim in late September of 1996, they were running on empty. The Mariners were chasing them down like a greyhound on a jackrabbit.

Some may say it was John Burkett's pitching that stopped the slide. Others will say that Ken Hill's win the next day was the key, bumping the Rangers' lead in the division back to two games. I wouldn't argue with either contention. But for me, it was Johnny Oates who breathed new life into a team that had stopped believing in itself.

He showed up at the ballpark with a smile as wide as Texas, and that changed everything.

Texas Rangers

Johnny Oates, pictured here with Pudge Rodríguez, led the Rangers to their first AL West title and playoff appearance in 1996.

Chapter 14

THE PRESS BOX
Competitors and Compadres

RANDY GALLOWAY was a damn shark.
I came to that realization as I began religiously following Rangers coverage in all three local papers a couple of years after the team arrived from Washington in 1972. Galloway was at the top of the food chain when it came to covering the Texas Rangers. His daily notes were crammed with juicy nuggets and news items that the other beat writers, including those at my own paper, the *Fort Worth Star-Telegram,* just didn't have.

It irritated the hell out of me.

I'd known Galloway since he'd arrived at the *Dallas Morning News* from the Port Arthur paper in 1966. I was 20 years old and just getting started in the business at the *Arlington News-Texan* (later the *Arlington Daily News*). We would run into each other at high school football games from time to time, and he was always more than willing to offer a helping hand. It was one of Galloway's best traits. (He had a few others, though, that always seemed to get me into trouble.)

"Mr. Randy," as he frequently referred to himself, was friendly with everyone, including but not limited to out-of-town writers, clubhouse boys, press box attendants, ticket takers, elevator operators, janitors and bartenders across the land, from San Francisco's Haight-Ashbury to New York's Hell's Kitchen.

I would learn from that template, too. I made it a personal mission to treat the clubhouse guys to dinner at least once each spring training I was on the beat. That didn't mean they were going to blurt secrets in my ear, but it never hurts to have someone remember that you were kind to them.

~ ~ ~

GALLOWAY HAD WORKED his way up from high school and college beats to cover the Dallas Chaparrals of the American Basketball Association (later to become the NBA's San Antonio Spurs) for two seasons. When major-league baseball arrived in 1972, *DMN* sports editor Walter Robertson had astutely paired Galloway with the paper's longtime minor-league baseball writer, Merle Heryford, as his first Rangers beat writers.

The crosstown rival *Dallas Times Herald* countered with its own longtime minor-league baseball man, Harry Gage, and sports editor Blackie Sherrod brought in David Fink from the Houston Post as his lead Rangers writer. It was one of Blackie's rare personnel misses. Fink was a hard worker, but he struggled to connect with the players. He lacked Galloway's flair and personality in the clubhouse. Then again, you could say the same about most of us.

The *Star-Telegram*'s first Rangers beat writers were Harold McKinney, who would appropriately have the team's "Good Guy Award" named for him after his untimely death from cancer in 1975, and former *Fort Worth Press* sportswriter and legendary free spirit Mike Shropshire. Shrop's greatest contribution to Rangers baseball would be his hilarious 20-years-after-the-fact book, *Seasons in Hell*, chronicling the team's 105-loss '73 season and its turnaround in '74.

How many of the tales Shropshire related were absolute truth or the result of his dipping generously into the grocery bag full of marijuana he confessed to bringing to spring training may be up for debate, but there was no doubt that the book was delightful and entertaining.

It was Galloway, though, who dominated the scene on the baseball beat right from the start, both in reporting and in personality. His easygoing, devil-may-care approach to life coupled with his heavy Texas drawl and razor-sharp wit were a knockout combination with players, owners and front-office executives. And his journalistic pursuit of inside information on the team was relentless.

Galloway would build a lucrative career out of bashing ownership, first as a Rangers beat writer and later as a general sports columnist and wildly popular radio talk-show host at WBAP and ESPN.

What was astonishing — and particularly discouraging to a competitor — was how he could blister Brad Corbett or Eddie Chiles in print one day, and the next they'd be smiling through their fury, slapping him on the back and cracking jokes with him. They so desperately wanted Randy to like them. The rest of us just wished they'd quit spilling their guts to him every time he called.

Back in 1972, though, that first season was new and challenging for all the writers.

"To be honest about it, I was scared to death," Galloway says 50 years after the fact. "I was scared of failure, scared I wasn't going to get it right. That motivated me. Coming in with [manager] Ted Williams, was I going to survive with this guy?

"He had a reputation as a guy who chewed up the media, but he could not have been nicer to me."

"Ted was fair to the Texas guys. We'd go to Boston, though — he'd growl and cuss at the writers there. They had a history. All of us [Rangers beat writers] were feeling our way, and none of us were hammering on the team much; maybe [owner] Bob Short a little bit."

~ ~ ~

THEN, IN EARLY April 1976, the *Star-Telegram* tossed a juicy morsel into those shark-infested waters — me. I was a naïve 29, but covering major-league baseball was all I'd ever wanted to do since I was 14, growing up on the Pecos River in southeastern New Mexico. The game fell on me like a fever in 1957 when I was enchanted by the Milwaukee Braves of Hank Aaron, Eddie Mathews and Warren Spahn. It was, I would discover, an incurable disease.

Almost 20 years later I would find myself driving from Pompano Beach, Fla., where the Rangers trained, to their minor-league camp at Plant City. I was working on some stories on the team's top prospects and discovered that Mathews, my all-time favorite player and a Rangers scout, was in town. He was happy to make a new friend with an expense account. Not as delighted as I was, however; I bought him all the whiskey he could drink that night.

It was a lot.

My dream of becoming a major-league baseball beat writer had unexpectedly come true when my sports editor called me at home one early April morning in 1976. "Pack your bags," he told me. "You're leaving with the Rangers tomorrow night."

Shropshire's lifelong habit of living on the edge had caught up with him again. He was out, and I was up to bat. It was definitely going to be a step up from covering North Texas football, TCU baseball and Golden Gloves.

It didn't even bother me that my first road trip as a baseball writer would be to the wildly popular vacation hotspots of Cleveland and Detroit. I loved them both.

We traveled like kings in those days. Rangers beat writers in the '70s were literally "embedded" with the team, traveling on team buses, flying on the same flights, staying at the same hotels.

When we arrived at the Hollenden House Hotel in downtown Cleveland, I followed Rangers traveling secretary Burt Hawkins and the other writers and broadcasters to the hotel bar. I nervously ordered a Scotch and soda. It might have been the first one I'd ever had. Hawk leaned across the table and spoke out of the corner of his mouth in his typical Humphrey Bogart style: "Buddy boy, pick yourself a good brand and stick with it; that bar Scotch will kill you."

Hawk's tip may have been the best advice anyone ever gave me. I was on my way as a major-league beat writer.

THE INCREDIBLE access we had to the manager, coaches and players helped us provide our newspaper readers real insight into who these people were beyond the statistics that ran every morning in the paper. Without that access our readers would never have known in 1975 that a drunken Billy Martin had slapped Burt Hawkins and threatened to throw him off the team's charter flight in midair after an argument over something as inane as Burt's wife Janet helping to start a Rangers' wives' club.

Hawk's pointed reply to the threat summed up Martin's tumultuous career in a nutshell — and demonstrates why the late, great Hawkins was one of my heroes: "If you do, Billy boy, I'll die with more dignity than you've ever shown."

That this happened in the plane's first-class cabin with *Dallas Times Herald* beat writer James Walker sitting directly behind Hawkins is even more astounding.

Not only did the writers travel on the team flights (which allegedly were billed back to the newspapers), we were in the same rotation as players and coaches when it came to who sat in the first-class cabin on charters and even commercial flights.

Don't ask; I can't explain the rationale.

There were times I would find myself in first class while team stars like Buddy Bell, Jim Sundberg or Al Oliver would be relegated to the back of the plane. It was nuts, but who was I to argue with an arrangement that had been in place for years?

The back of the plane was where all the fun was, though. I once accepted reliever Jim Kern's offer of $50 to swap my first-class seat for his coach seat on a seven-hour cross-country flight from Boston to Seattle (hey, 50 bucks was a lot of money back then). The irony: Kern spent the whole flight playing cards and yukking it up with his teammates back in coach.

Hanging with Galloway and the *Times Herald*'s Walker, a friend I'd briefly worked with in Tyler, was an eye-opening challenge. Walker was quieter than Galloway but determined and relentless. His first game as a Rangers beat writer a year earlier had been 10-Cent Beer Night in Cleveland, when the Rangers had been forced to fight their way back to the visiting clubhouse after thousands of fans charged the field in the ninth inning.

Galloway was omnipresent. His outsized personality dominated the press box. There were days I loved him and days when he was insufferable. Trying to keep up with him was suffocating, but I loved the competition and hated it when I was beaten on a story.

~ ~ ~

IT WAS an age of newspapering when "scoops" mattered, and the Rangers beat was fast becoming the most competitive arena in the local sports pages, maybe in the whole newspaper. At some point over the next few seasons, I gradually began holding my own. At least I felt I could breathe again.

Did the pressure ease up when Galloway was promoted to general sports columnist in 1982? Not a chance. Galloway was still at Arlington Stadium on a regular basis, and now he had reinforcements. The *Morning News* hired a diminutive firecracker from Baltimore named Tim Kurkjian as its beat man. You might know him today from his TV gigs as an ESPN analyst on "Baseball Tonight" and in the booth during games.

In December 2021, Kurkjian won the Baseball Writers of America Award for Career Excellence, a well-deserved honor. Tim and I would become fast friends — I was an usher at his wedding — but he was just as fierce a competitor as Galloway had been.

Standing maybe 5-foot-4 on his tiptoes, Tim is the kind of funny character you think you must have seen on a *Seinfeld* episode (in fact, one of his best friends, actor Matt McCoy, played Lloyd Braun on *Seinfeld*). When Kurkjian first arrived in Dallas, he was dispatched to the home of SMU football coach Ron Meyer to try to get an interview at the height of the team's cheating scandal in the 1980s. When tiny Tim rang the doorbell and said he was with the *Morning News,* Meyer turned to his wife and asked if she had money for the paperboy. Tim delighted in telling that story on himself.

Like Galloway's, Tim's unique personality was a terrific tool in developing sources. It's also why he's so refreshing as a baseball analyst on ESPN's game broadcasts and owns two Emmys for his TV work. Manager Doug Rader, for one, couldn't get enough of Tim's self-deprecating humor — and, since Rader despised the rest of us ... well, you can guess what that meant in terms of our access.

I had both the *Star-Telegram* and the *Morning News* delivered to my home; as soon as I was up, I would stumble sleepily into the front yard to grab the *Morning News* first to see if Galloway or Kurkjian had beaten me on something. It was always a relief when I had at least broken even so I could grab an extra hour's sleep. If not ... forget about sleep; the day was already ruined.

Besides Galloway and Kurkjian, I would become close friends with the *Times-Herald's* Paul Hagen, who followed Walker, as well as with his successors, Randy Youngman and then Phil Rogers.

It was a rare night on the road, in fact, when the beat writers from all three papers didn't convene at a friendly watering hole after games to wind down. At home, Smacko's, owned by popular Rangers home clubhouse manager Joe Macko, was a safe haven.

Baseball writers comprise a unique brotherhood. We shared the same trials and tribulations — facing off with an irate player or manager, screaming over the phone with a demanding copy editor, cussing out a telecopier or computer that had crashed right on deadline. We all fought hard for our small victories, but after deadline we wanted the company of the only ones who could truly understand — each other.

~ ~ ~

AFTER THE RANGERS' '86 season, I informed Bruce Raben, my sports editor at the *Star-Telegram,* that I was ready to step away from the daily grind of covering baseball after 11 full years on the beat. The paper had hired Hagen away from the *Times-Herald,* and together we'd just had a great season of Rangers coverage. It seemed like a good time to try something else.

The intense pressure of deadlines and relentless competition was taking its toll. I needed a change that would allow me to spend more time with my family. Raben graciously gave me the opportunity to write a couple of columns a week and do some feature writing.

A year later, Ellen Thornley (Alfano) became the *Star-Telegram's* first female sports editor, and she immediately made me a full-time columnist. I would do that for the next quarter of a century, until I retired from the paper in 2009.

As a side note, I worked for two amazing female sports editors, Alfano and Celeste Williams, in my 40 years at the *Star-Telegram.* Both left us far too soon. They were top of the line in talent, profession and leadership. Each of them made me a better reporter, writer and person. I owe them much. I loved them both.

I also had the opportunity to work under my friend and former *Times Herald* competitor James Walker. When the *Star-Telegram* was looking for a sports editor in 1978, I had heartily recommended him for the job. He was a great asset for me on the baseball beat because he had hands-on knowledge of its difficulties and challenges.

Raben came over from the *Morning* News and was driven to make the *Star-Telegram* sports section one of the best in the country. He pushed me to be the best reporter I could be. I knew that each morning when we talked, I needed to be prepared to discuss every aspect of what was going on with the Rangers. Bruce was at the office early, reading all three local sports sections from cover to cover. He took copious notes so that he could intelligently discuss everything about everyone's beat. He was the best-prepared sports editor I ever worked under.

~ ~ ~

IN 1987 I was asked if I would take on coverage of the upcoming sale of the Rangers as a special project. As I related in an earlier chapter, Eddie Chiles was looking to sell, and prospective buyers were surfacing.

Early in the process of trying to uncover the various groups kicking the tires on the club, as I've already noted, I had stumbled upon local real estate wheeler-dealer Dan Shackelford. Shackelford was hoping to broker a real estate deal for a new stadium as part of the Rangers sale. If I promised to keep his name out of it, Shackelford promised he would feed me inside information on the sale as it developed.

Shackelford's inside info, which proved to be amazingly accurate, helped the *Star-Telegram* dominate the sale coverage. That included breaking the story that a group led by the son of the president not only was interested in buying the team but was the leading candidate to be the Rangers' next owner.

The *Star-Telegram* nominated me for a Pulitzer Prize for my months-long coverage, which was flattering. I didn't make the list of finalists, but it felt a little like running last in the Kentucky Derby: At least you get to see Churchill Downs and sip a mint julep. In my case, it was a celebratory Shiner Bock.

Even though I was no longer at the ballpark every day after handing off the beat, I wouldn't get far from the Rangers over the next 25 years. I worked hand in hand with the *Star-Telegram*'s excellent line of baseball writers, including T.R. Sullivan, Tony DeMarco, Steve Campbell, Johnny Paul, Jeff Wilson and Anthony Andro.

T.R., also retired now, was a special collaborator and friend. He is a brilliant man with a great mind for the history of baseball, or anything else, for that matter. He had first been assigned to back up Tony DeMarco in 1990, but with the paper expanding baseball coverage, I recommended to Alfano that Tony become our national writer with T.R. taking over the beat in '91.

It turned out to be a great move on both fronts. Tony had good sources around baseball and a smooth, readable writing style. T.R., for his part, pounded the beat like an old-style newspaperman. All he needed was a fedora and a card that read "PRESS" stuck in the hatband. Nobody outworked T.R.

We established a terrific relationship that allowed us to develop story and column ideas and break news. There was nothing better than a late-night, post-game brainstorming session with T.R. You knew it was going to be a great evening when T.R. would tell the bartender, "Sprinkle the infield!" and wave for another round.

T.R. would spend 17 years on the Rangers beat in Fort Worth

and another 15 doing the same thing for MLB.com. His 32 combined years covering the team easily holds the record among Texas Rangers beat men.

SOMETIME EARLY in the summer of 1998 I was summoned to the newspaper for a meeting with sports editor Celeste Williams and managing editor Jim Witt. They had a question for me: Did I think Galloway might consider moving from the *Morning News* to the *Star-Telegram*? And if so, would I consider approaching him about it?

It was relatively common knowledge that there had been on-going tension between Randy and *Morning News* sports editor Dave Smith, but I'd heard they'd settled their differences. I wasn't convinced Galloway would leave "The Evil Empire," where he'd worked for 36 years, to come to Fort Worth. I certainly didn't mind asking, though.

When I did, the answer surprised me.

"Absolutely," Galloway said, "but only if it's something you and Gil are on board with, too."

Gil was Gil LeBreton, a superb wordsmith and the paper's senior sports columnist, and within a week he and I were with Galloway in a private box at The Ballpark, discussing in detail how this new arrangement might work among the three of us.

It would, we discovered over the next 15 or so years, work beautifully.

The Shark was finally swimming on our side of the Metroplex. It was safe for us at the *Star-Telegram* to go back in the water.

I HAD another huge surprise coming in the summer of 2016, seven years after I had retired from the *Star-Telegram*. Jeff Wilson, president of the local Baseball Writers Association of America chapter, phoned me in Costa Rica, where I was vacationing with family. He told me that I was one of three finalists for what was then the J.G. Taylor Spink Award for Meritorious Baseball Writing (now known as the Career Excellence Award). Winning the award includes a place in the media wing of the National Baseball Hall of Fame in Cooperstown, N.Y., an incredible honor.

I was floored. Lifetime baseball writers are the normal recipients of the award. Each BBWAA chapter nominates a candidate, and a three-person national committee picks three finalists from the 30 nominees. The award is voted on by the members, who number about 500, each fall.

I was a finalist for four straight years and was runner-up in the voting each time. I'm sure there's a bridesmaid joke there somewhere. I asked to be taken out of future consideration after that. For four straight years I lost out to incredibly talented and deserving baseball writers. I was humbled and honored to have been a finalist at all. It was never something I expected after choosing to become a general columnist instead of sticking exclusively with baseball writing. I have no regrets.

No regrets . . . that's a good way to wrap things up here. The reality is, I'm still that kid from a little town in southeastern New Mexico who somehow stumbled into a dream. I had the opportunity to cover 29 World Series, a dozen or so Super Bowls, NCAA football championships, the Final Four, the College World Series, world championship boxing, the Winter Olympics, the Stanley Cup finals, the British Open, the Tour de France . . . on and on.

I've interviewed Muhammad Ali, Michael Jordan and Joe DiMaggio. I've partied after Super Bowls with Troy Aikman, Emmitt Smith and Michael Irvin; I had the opportunity to become friends with the greatest high school basketball coach of all time, Fort Worth's own Robert Hughes.

I kissed Morganna the Kissing Bandit and sat on the same barstool that Billy Martin had occupied just before he was beaten to a pulp at the Arlington strip club Lace. I rode a cutting horse alongside Nolan Ryan and swam across a raging flood to help Bobby Valentine drag his son's drowned Welsh pony back to dry land. I watched Ali fight his penultimate fight in Las Vegas, wincing at every punch Larry Holmes landed.

I've accidentally stepped on actress Rebecca De Mornay's toes on press row at Caesar's Palace, rubbed elbows with Sylvester Stallone and Mr. T, chatted with a very young John Travolta as we watched a heavyweight championship bout at the MGM Grand.

And I danced to the Beach Boys on the ledge of the press box at Arlington Stadium.

Regrets? Are you kidding?

My only regret is that I can't do it all over again.

Chapter 15

POSTCARDS FROM THE LEDGE
Incidents and Escapades

*N*EVER AGAIN WILL BASEBALL *writers have the kind of access to managers, coaches and players my fellow sportswriters and I had in the '70s and most of the '80s. When the Rangers traveled, we rode with them on the team bus; flew with them on their flights; stayed in the same hotels. We ate our scrambled eggs elbow-to-elbow in the same coffee shops; downed our beers after games in the same bars, saloons, pubs, honky-tonks and discos.*

It could never happen today, in the age of cellphone video, Twitter and TMZ. But that was a different era, and it worked in part because of an unwritten rule — a tacit, unspoken arrangement — that had been passed down from generations of beat writers before us: If it doesn't happen between the white lines, thou shalt not spill the beans.

There were exceptions, of course. If the local constabulary became involved, all bets were off. Likewise, if the boys became a little too playful in the speakeasy of their choice and broken bones or missing teeth were the result, such developments could find their way into the next day's Rangers notes.

Basically, though, it was simple: If the off-field activities didn't involve the cops, or a player's ability to perform his on-field duties, the blissful readers of the local sports pages in Dallas and Fort Worth could sleep believing their heroes were choirboys.

No doubt the Keepers of the Journalistic Oath of Ethical Responsibility, Truth and the American Way are foaming at the mouth just about now, gnawing on their copies of the AP Stylebook and convulsing in indignant rage.

I get it — but can the noise for a minute.

Obviously, this cozy arrangement would never happen today. Newspapers of that era, however, welcomed the convenience and the economic advantages these traveling arrangements offered. For hacks like me, they also provided a grand opportunity to observe the elusive American Major League Baseball Player in his native habitat as he spread his plumage across this great land of ours.

We were around the players daily, which allowed them to become accustomed to seeing our faces: They knew who we were and could figure out over time whether we were trustworthy or wolves in creeps' clothing. Some grew to tolerate us. Some never would. One thing for sure, though, as the recollections that follow will make quite clear: We weren't strangers.

The incidents and escapades below are a few personal selections from my scrapbook of the years I spent embedded with the Texas Rangers.

MY WELCOME to the big leagues, back in 1974, wasn't exactly a trial by fire, but it gave me an idea of the kind of fortitude I'd need to be hanging with the players.

It came at the hands of journeyman catcher Duke Sims and out-fielder Jeff Burroughs. I'd been assigned to write a feature story on Burroughs, who was in the early stages of putting together an MVP season, so I had arranged to meet him in the home-team dugout a couple of hours before a game at Arlington Stadium.

What I didn't know was that Burroughs was perhaps the team's No. 1 practical joker at the time. And a young, naïve sportswriter was the perfect target.

Burroughs seemed to be in an especially festive mood as we settled down on the bench in the dugout. Moments later, just as I was getting my interview started, Sims wandered out from the clubhouse. I didn't suspect there was a purpose to his presence until Burroughs looked at me and said, "Ever seen a guy throw up on command?"

Then he turned to Sims and said, "Show him, Duke."

Just like that, Sims bent over and threw up into the dugout drain. It happened so fast I never had a chance to move. I just froze.

"Again!" Burroughs shouted.

A second gout of vomit splashed out. Feeling queasy, I scuttled to the other end of the dugout

Welcome to the big leagues, rook.

"Now, what'd you want to talk about?" Burroughs said, grinning at me.

It was a short interview.

~ ~ ~

RANDY GALLOWAY, who covered the Rangers for the *Dallas Morning News,* had a standing maxim that became standard operating procedure for most of us: Show up in the clubhouse on the day you ripped someone in the paper.

It was important that a player understood you would be there if he wanted to go postal on you. It wasn't fun for the sportswriters, but it was necessary for our credibility with the players.

Having a player suggest you do really humiliating things to yourself at the top of his voice while 24 other world-class athletes glare murderously in agreement is uncomfortable, for sure. But verbal abuse came with our jobs, just as it sometimes did for the players. If you dished it out in the newspaper, you'd best be prepared to handle the fallout in the clubhouse. The rationale was that the players would at least respect you for showing up to take the heat. I'm not sure that part ever really worked.

I do know that players had little respect for writers who *didn't* show up in the clubhouse to take their medicine. Skip Bayless, a columnist at the *Dallas Times Herald* and later the *Dallas Morning News* before going national, was one of those. Several times players asked me why Bayless never came into the clubhouse.

Clearly, they had something profound they wanted to say to him. I could only shrug and explain that Skip apparently preferred to dish his jabs from afar and was likely sipping a chilled chardonnay somewhere as we spoke.

There were a few occasions over the years when reactions to what we'd written threatened to progress beyond mere harsh language and baleful looks.

One of these, for me, involved Jimmy Piersall, a former major-league player whose treatment for bipolar disorder had been detailed in his autobiography "Fear Strikes Out," later made into a movie. The movie, in which he was portrayed by actor Anthony Perkins of "Psycho" fame, at one point showed Piersall climbing the screen behind home plate at Fenway Park, trying to get to the fans who were taunting him.

Late in the '76 season, I had written a story in which I had asked Rangers owner Brad Corbett about manager Frank Lucchesi's status for the '77 season (he would be fired in June of that year). Piersall, a Corbett lackey at the time, got prickly about my line of questioning.

Standing in front of the visiting dugout in Oakland, Piersall loudly accused me of trying to get Lucchesi fired. I told him, in my usual genteel manner, that he was full of it. Piersall, living up to his reputation, went into a rage, circling me in a frenzy and screaming at the top of his voice as if I'd just nicked the last beer at the bar.

Back in '74, the same thing had happened to my colleague Mike Shropshire, and Shrop, always Mr. Cool, had casually dropped one of his killer lines on Piersall:

"I've seen your movie."

Since Shrop had already zinged him with the best possible comeback of all, I was searching my brain for a cool mike-drop line of my own when Lucchesi himself intervened, escorting the raging Piersall back into the clubhouse and allowing me to escape to the press box mostly unscathed, if you don't count bleeding eardrums.

Lucchesi was invariably a nice man.

~ ~ ~

SOMETHING ABOUT Oakland in September seemed to unleash the demonic in folks, but then, I often felt the same way after eating Charlie Finley's Kentucky Fried Chicken in the media lounge there. I was sitting in that same visiting dugout a few hours before game time a couple years later, trying to decipher the scribbles in my notebook, when suddenly an explosion seemed to go off beside my left ear.

When my eyes uncrossed, I realized that Toby Harrah, clearly unhappy with my smartass writing style, had planted his left foot, bristling with what appeared to be razor-sharp cleats, flat against the wall beside my ear with such precision I doubted I'd have to shave that side of my jaw for a month.

"Jimmy," Toby asked in a reasonably calm voice considering the mayhem he was obviously contemplating, "why are you such an asshole?"

It was the "Jimmy" that let me know Toby was being very serious. I assumed it was a rhetorical question, which was expedient, since no good answer sprang immediately to mind. I did grasp why Toby was upset. With the 1978 season winding down, I had picked at him unmercifully in print. It was another disappointing end to a season that had begun with great promise, and I suppose I wasn't handling it well. Toby had been bearing the brunt of my disgruntlement.

After hitting 27 homers with 87 RBIs and a league-leading 109 walks in '77, Toby had slumped to .229/12/59 in '78, and I had gone out of my way to point out how he had underperformed. Hindsight tells me I may have been a bit overzealous in my critiques.

I like Toby — I even named one of my cats after him some years ago (I liked to confuse the cat by sometimes calling him "Colbert Dale," Toby's real first and middle names; I don't think the cat ever got it). Since those youthful days, I've come to the conclusion that Toby Harrah was a better all-around player in his career than he ever got credit for being. The analytics nerds would love him today, with his ability to hit for power, steal bases and draw more walks than strike-outs.

I especially appreciated him in his second tour with the Rangers, and as interim manager after Bobby Valentine was fired. He deserved better from me. I've told him that a few times, too, but I'm not sure that it soothed the hurt feelings much.

Distance and a bit more maturity tell me now that Toby was right; I was being an a-hole. Thankfully, Toby knew exactly where to put that foot. I only had to rearrange my pants, not my profile, when all was said and done. No blood, no foul.

～ ～ ～

IN THE EARLY '80s there was another incident with a player that threatened to get physical, and again it was someone I liked a lot. I had offered some criticism of Billy Sample's ability to play left field, and it didn't make him or his wife happy. She wrote a letter to the sports editor, complaining about my disparagement of her husband's defensive talents, or lack thereof.

It was a well-worded missive, even if I did find it somewhat bi-ased. I'd just read it that morning and was brooding about it when I crossed paths with Billy near the batting cage before the game that night. Being young and dumb, I snidely asked Billy, a graduate of James Madison University, if he'd dictated the letter or if his bride had penned it on her own. Admittedly, the barb didn't meet the standards of my usual clever repartee.

Next thing I knew, Billy and I were chin-to-chin, exchanging a variety of colorful unpleasantries. Suddenly, Rangers first-base coach Fred Koenig was waltzing me backwards, while manager Don Zimmer was doing the same with Sample.

Until then, I hadn't realized what a kerfuffle we were causing. Koenig and Zimmer had interpreted our body language as an indication of imminent violence, which was certainly never my intention, since we all know how that would have turned out. That was not my kind of dancing.

Never had I been happier to see Koenig's placid countenance fill my vision. I determined then and there that the next time I was in Hank's on the Hill, the popular post-game hangout, I would light a candle for him ... or buy him a beer, whichever came first. Cooler heads had indeed prevailed, which was appropriate, since both Koenig and Zim were as bald as brand-new cue balls.

~ ~ ~

ANOTHER MEMORABLE contretemps involved Brad Corbett, Fort Worth's self-made plastic-pipe millionaire who owned the Rangers from 1974 to 1980.

You could call Brad Corbett a larger-than-life personality. Brad was a caricature, loud, flamboyant, outsized. He was the ringmaster at the circus — everything revolved around him.

Here Brad is, shirttail caught in his fly, holding court in the Arlington Stadium press lounge — waving his arms, a dripping beef rib in one hand, a vodka tonic in the other, barbecue sauce dribbling down his chin. Or there he goes, emotionally calling his players "dogs, on and off the field," threatening to sell the Rangers to "a bunch of Arabs."

Texas Rangers

Brad Corbett owned the Rangers from 1974-1980.

In fact, you never knew what Brad Corbett might say from one moment to the next, so it was imperative to be the last reporter to talk to him every day.

The nickname the great Texas writer Gary Cartwright coined for Corbett in an article for *Texas Monthly* magazine in the mid-'70s was "Chuckles the Clown." It was so cute I repeated it in one of my own columns.

Up to that point, my relationship with Brad had been in line with his general mercurial temperament: Sometimes he loved me; other times he was marching down to the *Star-Telegram* offices to have me fired on the spot. Fortunately, the publisher kept shooing him out of the office.

But when I borrowed Cartwright's "Chuckles the Clown" zinger, something snapped with Brad. Seeing it in his hometown newspaper must have been a bit embarrassing for him, especially when it seemed to stick. During that night's game at the stadium, I received a summons to meet him in club president Eddie Robinson's office. I grabbed my notebook and went to meet my fate.

When I walked in, Brad furiously slammed the door behind me and started screaming. He was trying to keep his cigar in his mouth, and his face was turning a deep purple. Spittle and bits of tobacco were flying everywhere. The only words I could understand were "DON'T EVER CALL ME CHUCKLES THE CLOWN AGAIN!"

Unnerved at the sight of a grown man on the verge of apoplexy, I stepped over and reopened the office door. My friend Debbie Cartwright (no relation to Gary) was at the reception desk just outside, and I wanted a witness in case Brad, a large man teetering on the brink of madness, decided to wring my neck like a Sunday-dinner chicken's.

With an escape route now open, I turned and yelled back at Corbett, a move that can be added to a long list of questionable decisions in my life.

Brad gritted his teeth, almost biting his cigar in half, gathered himself and stalked back to his private box across the hall with me nipping at his heels like a depraved Chihuahua. Debbie warily eyed the two of us as if we'd just escaped from the psychiatric hospital down the street.

A few weeks later, before the last home game of the season, I got a call from my sports editor. Someone identifying himself as a friend of Corbett's had phoned the paper's switchboard several times with the same ominous message: "If Jim Reeves shows up at the ballpark tonight, he won't be going home."

The threats made the paper's editors nervous. I was told I didn't have to cover that night's game. Nope, I said, nobody was going to keep me from my rendezvous with John Denver and the Cotton-Eyed Joe. Besides, the Rangers were kind enough to assign a police officer to keep me company in the press box — although I was disappointed when he declined to bring me a hot dog and a Miller Lite during the seventh-inning stretch.

~ ~ ~

CORBETT AND I settled into an uneasy truce after he sold the Rangers to Eddie Chiles, but I realized that perhaps Brad still harbored some ill feelings on the night that Don Zimmer was fired as Rangers manager.

Some of us had arranged for an impromptu private farewell party for Zimmer at Mr. Catfish. We were toasting Zim and swapping stories when Corbett made a surprise appearance to pay his respects.

Hands were being shaken and backs were being slapped when he spotted me at the other end of the table. He never stopped grinning, but he hauled off and fired his glass of beer in the general direction of my head.

With a melon like mine, I'm not sure how he missed. Fortunately, though, Brad Corbett was no Fergie Jenkins.

~ ~ ~

OF ALL THE flakes the Rangers have employed over the years, Jim Kern ranks in the top five. His tall, gangly physique and goofy hairstyle were just part of the reason he was tagged with the nickname "The Amazing Emu."

Still with Cleveland at the time, he happened to be walking by pitchers Pat Dobson and Fritz Peterson in the clubhouse when they were working a crossword and temporarily stumped. The clue to the three-letter word they were searching for was "the largest non-flying bird." They looked up to see Kern standing there. "Emu," they both said simultaneously.

Kern ambled away, flapping his elbows like short little wings. And just like that, a new persona was born.

Kern took the nickname and ran with it. He began using it to complement his one great talent — throwing a fastball — with a touch of insanity, with a view toward eroding the hitters' confidence.

"The Amazing Emu" was a full-blown character by the time he arrived in Texas in 1979. With Kern anchoring the bullpen and often pitching multiple innings, the Rangers were 31-24 and in second place in the American League West when they got to Baltimore on June 8. Kern was 7-1 with a league-leading 1.20 ERA.

Then things began to sour. Left-hander Mike Flanagan shut out the Rangers 3-0 on four hits in the first game of the series. A ninth-inning rally fell a run short in Game 2, and the Rangers lost 4-3. But Game 3 brought the real heartbreaker.

The Rangers built a 4-2 lead behind starter Jon Matlack, but when Eddie Murray led off with a double in the bottom of the ninth, manager Pat Corrales brought in his closer to seal the deal. It was the logical move, but Kern immediately walked Gary Roenicke.

Kern and third baseman Buddy Bell expected a bunt from big Lee May. The plan was for Bell to charge the bunt unless Kern, who would be covering the middle of the field, could pounce on it quickly, in which case Bell would retreat to third base for the throw. If Bell had to make the play, he would concede the advancing runners and throw to first for the out there.

May bunted the ball down the third-base line. Kern, a little too athletic for his own good, came almost all the way to the line to snatch the ball and throw to third. Just then he heard a voice say, "Kernie! No!"

He turned to find Bell standing beside him. No one was on third, and the ball was rattling around the fence toward the left-field corner. Murray scored. Pinch-runner Al Bumbry wound up at third with May at second.

It was the beginning of a three-run walk-off rally that handed the O's a 5-4 victory and the series sweep.

Heading home with the team, I settled into my seat on the plane, wondering if this was the type of loss that could linger in the team's psyche for weeks. Would it break Kern's confidence? Could "The Amazing Emu" survive such a catastrophe?

The answer came far quicker than I could imagine. I had pulled out the book I'd been reading for weeks, John Dean's "Blind Ambition." I was on the last chapter, down to the final five or six pages, when suddenly the book was snatched out of my hands. I looked up to see Kern's smiling face looming over me.

I reached to take the book back, and Kern flipped it to Sparky Lyle, in the aisle several rows up. When I rose to pursue Lyle, he tossed the book back to Kern. It was classic keep-away, with me in the middle.

I charged Kern. He fended me off with one arm, ripped the last four pages out of the book … and ate them as I stood there gaping.

The whole plane — it was a commercial flight — seemed to think the stunt was hilarious. Me? Not so much.

Having almost finished the book, I didn't want to buy another copy, so I had to sneakily read the last four pages standing in a bookstore back in Texas.

Kern told me the last four pages tasted great but could have used a little Tabasco.

I didn't worry about his psyche after that.

THINGS COULD get even wilder if the Rangers were traveling by bus instead of by plane. It was rare, but the team used buses occasionally if the next stop wasn't too far away — say, from Cleveland to Detroit. The Rangers would employ two buses for the 3½-hour jaunt, and for many players (and the beat writers) the trick was to figure out which bus the manager would be on and land a seat on the other one.

The buses were loaded with coolers containing a splendid variety of fermented beverages to keep the players occupied and happy. The rationale was simple: There was a professional driver at the wheel and, besides, how loaded could these well-tuned athletes get in a mere three hours?

It should indeed have been a simple and relatively sober drive, taking the freeway west around the shores of Lake Erie and then north up to Detroit. The manager's bus made the trip exactly as planned, pulling up to the Detroit Plaza Hotel in the enormous Renaissance Center complex in record time.

On the second bus, however — the one I was on, along with some of the team's thirstier players — the driver made an unfortunate navigational error. Instead of going west, he headed south in the direction of Columbus, or perhaps the mountains of West Virginia.

It was my old pal Jim Kern who realized we were drastically off course. If Kern, who grew up in Michigan and had previously served time in Cleveland, hadn't awakened from a snooze and peeked out the bus window, we might have found ourselves following Sherman's march through Georgia.

As it was, what was supposed to have been a three-to-four-hour trip turned into a seven-hour mobile frathouse party and necessitated a panty raid on an unsuspecting McDonald's. At least that's what it seemed like. Imagine 20 well-oiled ballplayers and assorted others descending on Mickey D's like a flock of vultures on roadkill. First baseman Pat Putnam returned to the bus with a half-dozen bags of burgers and fries along with three milkshakes and threatened mayhem to anyone who thought he intended to share.

From the perspective of the poor bus driver, who had absorbed a barrage of verbal abuse for his directional misstep, the stop was a strategic success. By then the coolers had mostly run dry, and the food, on top of the alcohol, eventually lulled most of the passengers into a temporary coma.

Alas, another problem blossomed: The tiny restroom in the rear of the bus was not built to withstand a six-hour assault by a few dozen beer-swilling, Big-Mac-gulping 25-year-olds. At some point, as eyes began to water from the miasma emanating from the rear, there was a scramble for empty seats nearer the front of the old Greyhound.

~ ~ ~

IT'S REMARKABLE, when I think about it, how many of my best Rangers memories involve music.

The first time I met Charley Pride, he was wearing nothing but black silk boxer shorts and rubbing the sleep out of his eyes.

I'd answered the door to my room at the somewhat-less-than-five-star Surf Rider Hotel in Pompano Beach, Fla., to find him standing in front of it, looking a bit confused and trying to peer into my room over my shoulder.

"Are there termites or something in here?" he asked.

"I keep hearing this clicking sound," he said. "Click, click, click."

It dawned on me that the sound he was hearing was me tapping away on my portable Underwood typewriter as I wrapped up my dispatches back to the home front from the spring-training home of the Texas Rangers. I realized that Charley, a die-hard Rangers fan, must have the room next door to mine.

It was mid-February 1978, and I had heard that Charley had become a spring-training fixture with the Rangers, but this was our first encounter. It was only 9:30 at night, but obviously he'd been sleeping — or trying to sleep — while I was hurrying to finish my story for the morning paper so I could join the nightly gathering of writers, coaches and players in the Banyan Room — think cheesy Bill-Murray-style-crooner lounge — downstairs.

Fast-forward 25 years and 2,000 miles west, to a bright sunny morning and an empty Surprise Stadium, where the Rangers and Kansas City Royals now shared a shiny new spring-training complex surrounded by the red-sand hills of the Arizona desert. Charley Pride was back in the Rangers' camp, but he wasn't the only country-music megastar on site. Garth Brooks was working out with the Royals as part of his Teammates for Kids Foundation.

The idea seemed like a natural for a great column. While the Rangers and Royals were practicing on the back fields, why not bring Charley and Garth together to say hello in the big stadium? Fifteen minutes or so would be all we needed. Just the two stars, a sports columnist captivated by their music and a photographer to document the moment.

That said, I was attempting this without involving the PR folks for either team. Charley wasn't a problem, since we'd had a relationship since that long-ago night at the Surf Rider. I approached him on my own. As for Garth, my "in" was with former Rangers catcher Mark Parent, who was acting as driver and helper while the country star was in Arizona.

As it turned out, both singers jumped at the opportunity to get together wearing baseball uniforms.

The best part of the whole morning? When they each started singing snippets of each other's songs, a cappella, of course.

Garth started out with a line from Charley's "Kiss an Angel Good Morning." Charley countered with a beauty, Garth's "If Tomorrow Never Comes."

As Charley sang out on that glorious spring day in an almost-empty stadium, the three of us standing between the mound and home plate, Garth leaned over to me and whispered, "Isn't that beautiful?"

Indescribable, really. The confluence of the two iconic stars in that gorgeous setting — the vivid colors of their uniforms, the lush green infield grass, the red-dirt basepaths, the surrounding desert mountains — along with the purity of their voices, each so recognizable, was indescribably magical. It was as if a piece of priceless art had come to life to produce one of the most unforgettable and satisfying days in my 40-plus years of covering Rangers baseball.

~ ~ ~

DID I MENTION that I enjoyed the occasional boogie-woogie? If there were a band and a dance floor in the vicinity, the Dancing Bear was likely to be enthusiastically living up to his nickname.

This was common knowledge among the Rangers, since we all gathered at the same clubs on our travels. There were times when some of the players — those who may not have been as uninhibited on the dance floor as I was — decided my excess energy could be useful to them.

When the band started up at the club, they'd be sitting awkwardly at their tables, staring into their beers. Meanwhile, the sweet young things hovering around them were grooving to the music and raring to dance.

Now and then a player would shuffle over to me and mumble something like, "How about dancing with my woman?" I was happy to oblige. I became a warm-up act, if you get my drift.

My love of dancing would lead to an incident that became somewhat legendary in Rangers lore. I danced on the ledge at Arlington Stadium.

It was late in the '81 season, and the Oakland A's were in town. More importantly, so were the Beach Boys, who had been booked for a post-game concert. I loved the Beach Boys, so for me covering the game that night was simply a prelude to the main event. A few cold ones helped get me in the proper frame of mind.

I was still wrapping up my game story in the press box when Brian Wilson and the boys struck the first chords to "Help Me, Rhonda," but I was on my feet, dancing and typing at the same time. As soon as I hit "send" on my computer, I was in full party mode.

The press box windows had already been flung open, and I immediately saw that many of the paying customers in the private suites were hanging out of their windows. Some were sitting in the windows, with their legs dangling over the ledge that ringed the stadium maybe a dozen feet above the second deck.

Great idea, I thought. I climbed up on the counter that ran the length of the press box and stepped out onto the foot-wide ledge, holding on to the window jamb with one hand and a Miller Lite with the other. The Beach Boys moved on to "Barbara Ann," and once again I danced like nobody was watching ... except for the 25,000 or so Beach Boys fans who had no trouble spotting me on the big video screen in center field. They thought my act was hilarious.

Emboldened, I decided to dance my way down the ledge and into the open windows of owner Eddie Chiles' private box a few doors down (Eddie, wife Fran and friends had already departed). Meanwhile, a dozen feet below, security guards had arrived and had a succinct message for me: GET THE HELL DOWN FROM THERE, YOU IDIOT!

Sure enough, the gendarmes were waiting when I climbed through the window and into Chiles' suite. So was Bob Beamon, our head press box attendant.

"I'll take care of him!" Bob declared authoritatively. He sounded as if he were about to extract my toenails with rusty pliers. The security guards put away their tasers, and Bob ushered me safely back to the press box, where he asked if I wanted another beer. I'll always owe Bob, now patrolling that Press Box in the Sky, for that one.

I was amused the next day when I received a note from the managing editor, congratulating me for a "great lede" to my game story.

And from that adventurous evening sprang the idea for a name for my new Sunday *Star-Telegram* notes column: "Postcards From the Ledge."

When The Ballpark in Arlington was built, it was definitively decreed that the press box would not have windows that would open.

Now you know why.

In my dreams, I'm still dancing on that ledge.

ABOUT THE AUTHOR

JIM "REVO" REEVES, a much-lauded sports reporter and columnist at the *Fort Worth Star-Telegram* over four decades, covered 29 World Series, a dozen Super Bowls and numerous NBA championships and Stanley Cup Finals. He was the *Star-Telegram*'s Texas Rangers beat reporter for 10 years and continued to cover the team closely over 25 years while writing his award-winning column.

During his career in daily journalism, he was named Texas Sports Columnist of the Year on multiple occasions by both the Associated Press Managing Editors Association and the Associated Press Sports Editors Association. In 1987 he was nominated for a Pulitzer Prize for his coverage of the sale of the Texas Rangers to a group headed by future president George W. Bush. He is the only sportswriter ever to be honored with the national TCU Schieffer School of Journalism Ethics Award, in 2007, and was a four-time finalist for the Baseball Writers' Association of America Career Excellence Award.

Jim Reeves with Johnny Oates.

After retiring from the *Star-Telegram*, he wrote an ESPN.com column and now completes assignments for the *Texas Rangers Yearbook* and other publications.

Reeves is the author of "Dallas Cowboys: The Legends of America's Team" and "Remember the Alamo Bowl: Bram Kohlhausen's Epic TCU Comeback," both published by Great Texas Line Press.

He and his wife Karen live in Dalworthington Gardens, Texas.

A RANGERS TIMELINE

1960: The American League awards a new Major League Baseball franchise, the Washington Senators, to Washington, D.C.; the original club had been transferred to Minnesota and became the Twins.

1971: Senators owner Robert E. Short agrees to move the team to Arlington, Texas. To lure the team, 10 local banks have offered $7.5 million in low-interest loans and Mayor Tom Vandergriff has pledged $7.5 million from the City of Arlington for the team's broadcast rights and use of the community's minor-league stadium. Baseball icon Ted Williams continues as manager of the team, which is renamed the Texas Rangers.

Al Panzera, Courtesy, Fort Worth Star-Telegram Collection, Special Collections, The University of Texas at Arlington Libraries

David Clyde's debut on June 27, 1973, drew a capacity crowd to Arlington Stadium.

1972: The Rangers beat the California Angels 7-6 in the team's first home opener April 21 in Arlington Stadium; Vandergriff throws out the first pitch. **In November**, Whitey Herzog replaces Williams as manager.

1973: On June 5, the Rangers choose 18-year-old Texas native David Clyde, fresh from Houston's Westchester High School, as the first overall pick in the first round of the amateur draft. On June 27, Clyde takes the mound in Arlington Stadium, just 20 days after pitching his last high-school game. With more than 35,000 fans packing the stadium and

10,000 more turned away at the gates, it marks the first sellout for the Rangers. **In September,** Billy Martin becomes the third manager of the Rangers, signing on shortly after being fired by the Detroit Tigers and taking over from interim manager Del Wilber after he steps in for one game.

1974: A group led by Fort Worth plastic-pipe manufacturer Bradford G. Corbett buys the team for $9.5 million and assumes more than $1 million in debts.

1975: Frank Lucchesi is named manager.

1977: On March 28, player Len Randle punches Lucchesi, breaking a bone in the manager's face and sending him to the hospital for five days. The team suspends Randle for a month, fines him $10,000 and trades him to the Mets. Lucchesi's personal-injury suit is eventually settled out of court. **On May 8,** a 20-minute melee fracas erupts between the Rangers and the Kansas City Royals at Arlington Stadium, with skirmishes breaking out all over the field. **In June,** Lucchesi is replaced as manager by Eddie Stanky, who quits after one game. Third-base coach Connie Ryan becomes interim manager for six games before Billy Hunter is hired as manager.

Larry C. Price, Courtesy, Fort Worth Star-Telegram Collection, Special Collections, The University of Texas at Arlington Libraries

1978: Pitcher Roger Moret, holding a shower shoe, falls into a catatonic state in front of his locker in the Rangers clubhouse.

Catcher Jim Sundberg argues a call with umpire Vic Voltaggio in 1982.

Al Panzera, Courtesy, Fort Worth Star-Telegram Collection, Special Collections, The University of Texas at Arlington Libraries

Tom Grieve, second from right, whose home run beat the California Angels on July 27, 1973, went on to become the Rangers general manager at 36 in 1984.

1979: Pat Corrales becomes manager for the season's final game, becoming the team's fifth manager in two seasons.

1980: Fort Worth oilman and TV pitchman Eddie "If you don't own an oil well, get one" Chiles buys controlling interest in the team. Don Zimmer is named manager.

1981: An MLB strike shortens the MLB season.

1982: Darrell Johnson becomes interim manager July 28 and is replaced Nov. 1 by Doug Rader.

1984: At 36, former player Tom Grieve becomes Rangers general manager, MLB's youngest GM at the time.

1985: Bobby Valentine is hired to manage the Rangers 32 games into the season. Valentine will eventually become one of the team's longest-serving managers, with 1,186 games.

1988: Pitcher Nolan Ryan leaves the Houston Astros for the Rangers on Dec. 7.

1989: On March 18, a group fronted by George W. Bush, later to be-come Texas governor and the 43rd president, buys controlling interest of the team for $25 million and assumes $9 million in debt. With the purchase of Arlington Stadium and nearby property, the investment amounts to about $89 million. **On Aug. 22,** Nolan Ryan records his 5,000th career strikeout, be-coming the first and only player in MLB history to do so.

June 11, 1990: Ryan throws his sixth career no-hitter, in Oakland.

May 1, 1991: Ryan throws a no-hitter with 16 strikeouts against the Toronto Blue Jays in a 3-0 win at home — his seventh career no-hitter, more than any other pitcher in MLB history.

1992: In July, Toby Harrah becomes interim and then full-time man-ager but is replaced by Kevin Kennedy in October.

1994: On April 1, the 49,115-seat Ballpark at Arlington opens; the team wins its first division title. **On Aug. 4,** with Nolan Ryan

Ron Jenkins, Courtesy, Fort Worth Star-Telegram Collection, Special Collections, The University of Texas at Arlington Libraries

Nolan Ryan's teammates lift him on their shoulders after his record seventh no-hitter against the Toronto Blue Jays at Arlington Stadium on May 1, 1991.

Texas Rangers

Former manager Ron Washington, left, with then-GM Jon Daniels and former owner Tom Hicks, led the Rangers to their only World Series appearances, in 2010 and 2011.

pitching, Robin Ventura charges the mound and Ryan puts the Chicago White Sox player in a headlock. Ventura is ejected; Ryan is not. For the rest of the game, the crowd chants, "Nolan!" **In August,** the Rangers are leading the AL West with a record of 52 wins and 62 losses when another players' strike cancels the World Series and postseason games. In October, Johnny Oates becomes manager.

1996: Led by Oates, the Rangers win the American League Western Division championship, taking longer than any other North American team to do so — in their 36th season, 24 years after moving to Texas. Oates is named AL manager of the year.

1998: Oates leads the team to the American League West championships in 1998. A group led by Dallas venture capitalist Tom Hicks buys the team for $250 million. Bush's investment of just $606,000 — mostly borrowed — reportedly nets him $14.9 million.

1999: Oates leads the Rangers to another American League West championship. For $22.2 million, Hicks settles an eminent-do-main lawsuit for property acquired from heirs of TV tycoon Curtis Mathes Jr.

2000: Rangers sign free agent Alex Rodriguez in a widely criticized $252 million contract — $2 million more than Hicks had paid for the whole club. (Hicks, also owner of the Dallas Stars hockey team, is flush from signing a $550 million broadcast deal with Fox.)

2001: Jerry Narron becomes manager.

2002: Buck Showalter is named manager at the end of the season.

2004: Showalter is named AL manager of the year.

2005: At 28, Jon Daniels becomes general manager of the Rangers, the youngest GM in MLB history.

2006: Ron Washington is named manager, the franchise's first African-American to hold the position. Washington will become its winningest manager ever, with a 644-611 (.521) record and two World Series appearances in eight seasons.

2008: Nolan Ryan is named team president.

2010: The team files for Chapter 11 bankruptcy protection after Hicks' sports company defaults on loans totaling $525 million. A group including Nolan Ryan and Chuck Greenberg, backed by businessmen Bob Simpson and Ray Davis, pays $593 million to beat a bid by Mavericks owner Mark Cuban and future Houston Astros owner Jim Crane. **On Oct. 22,** the Rangers win their first American League pennant, and on Nov. 1 the team loses its first World Series, going down 4-1 against the San Francisco Giants.

2011: Chuck Greenberg resigns as CEO; Ryan becomes a minority owner and CEO while continuing as team president. The

Rangers make it to the World Series again and twice come within one strike of winning it all in Game 6, only to wind up losing to the St. Louis Cardinals in extra innings. The Cardinals make the comeback complete by easily winning Game 7 over the deflated Rangers.

2013: Nolan Ryan resigns as team CEO and sells his stake to Davis and Simpson. Jon Daniels, Rangers president of baseball operations and general manager, becomes operating head of the franchise.

2014: Bench coach Tim Bogar is selected manager in September for the remainder of the season when Ron Washington abruptly resigns. In October, Jeff Banister is named manager.

2015: Banister is named AL manager of the year.

Texas Rangers

Neil Leibman, Rangers president of business operations and chief operating officer, left, is joined by owners Bob Simpson and Ray Davis, former Arlington mayor Richard Greene and then-mayor Jeff Williams as the team moves home plate to the new Globe Life Field on the last day of the 2019 season.

2018: Another bench coach, Don Wakamatsu, takes over as interim manager for the season's last 10 games after Banister is dismissed.

2019: Chris Woodward becomes manager.

2020: The Covid-delayed, 60-game season starts July 24 at the new Globe Life Field; the Rangers down the Colorado Rockies 1-0. On Dec. 7, former player Chris Young becomes general manager as Daniels is promoted to president of baseball operations.

2021: The Rangers mark their 50th anniversary in Texas.

Sources: "Texas Rangers Master Timeline," Texas Rangers Baseball; *Fort Worth Star-Telegram*; *Dallas Observer;* special thanks to John Blake.